Reconciliation and Architectures of Commitment

Sequencing peace in Bougainville

Reconciliation and Architectures of Commitment

Sequencing peace in Bougainville

**John Braithwaite, Hilary Charlesworth,
Peter Reddy and Leah Dunn**

ANU

THE AUSTRALIAN NATIONAL UNIVERSITY

E PRESS

ANU

E PRESS

Published by ANU E Press
The Australian National University
Canberra ACT 0200, Australia
Email: anuepress@anu.edu.au
This title is also available online at: http://epress.anu.edu.au/bougainville_citation.html

---

National Library of Australia
Cataloguing-in-Publication entry

Title: Reconciliation and architectures of commitment : sequencing peace in
              Bougainville / John Braithwaite ... [et al.].

ISBN: 9781921666681 (pbk.) 9781921666698 (ebook)

Notes: Includes bibliographical references and index.

Subjects: Bougainville Crisis, Papua New Guinea, 1988-
              Women and peace--Papua New Guinea--Bougainville Island.
              Bougainville Island (Papua New Guinea)--History.
              Bougainville Island (Papua New Guinea)--Autonomy and independence
              movements.
              Bougainville Island (Papua New Guinea)--Politics and government.

Other Authors/Contributors:
              Braithwaite, John.

Dewey Number: 327.172099592

Cover design and layout by ANU E Press

Cover image: *Children of Resistance and Bougainville Revolutionary Army sides of the conflict
arrive at the signing of the Bougainville Ceasefire Agreement in Arawa wearing traditional upi
headdresses.* Photo: AAP/AFP Torsten Blackwood

Printed by Griffin Press

Contents

Acknowledgments

Australian Research Council (ARC) Federation Fellowships at The Australian National University supported John Braithwaite and Hilary Charlesworth to plan and read for the Peacebuilding Compared project. ARC Discovery grants then funded its execution. Our thanks are due to Kate Macfarlane who has done a splendid job in taking over from Leah Dunn as manager of the Peacebuilding Compared project. Kate's careful research and data-management contributions were vital to getting the job finished, as were those of Celeste Ecuyer, Charlie Beauchamp-Wood, Scott Rutar, Karina Pelling and Nick Kitchin.

Leah Dunn is a co-author of this book, though she also must be thanked for serving generously in the same capacity as Kate Macfarlane for many years. She participated in two fieldwork trips to Bougainville in which, among other things, she organised a Peacebuilding Conference on the occasion of the second anniversary of the Autonomous Bougainville Government in 2007. The conference was attended throughout two days plus preparatory meetings by the then President, Joseph Kabui, and his successor, President James Tanis, and also by the then Papua New Guinea Minister for Bougainville Affairs, Sir Peter Barter. These leaders have been iterative contributors to this research and to the peace in Bougainville. The conference was also graced by the participation of senior Me'ekamui participants who agreed to a most constructive communiqué drafted consultatively by President Tanis. Leah's video of the entire proceedings of the conference can be viewed online at <http://peacebuilding.anu.edu.au/videolib/index.php>.

Thanks to our ANU E Press series editor, Margaret Thornton, managers Lorena Kanellopoulos and Duncan Beard, and copy editor, Jan Borrie. Their wonderful publishing model means this book is available free on the Internet and also at a modest price as a handsome hardcopy. This is a special virtue for research of which the important readers are in developing countries. We are also grateful to the helpful suggestions made by the anonymous referees.

Our Advisory Panel members were invaluable in assisting with contacts to interview, publications to read and providing sophisticated commentary on drafts as well as other forms of advice. Many were extraordinarily generous with their time. Of course, they bear no responsibility for the interpretive and factual errors that remain in the final text.

Fieldwork for the book was conducted by John Braithwaite with Peter Reddy in 2006, building on earlier fieldwork on Peter's PhD on Bougainville (not included in the summary of the types of interviews listed in the Appendix; Reddy 2006) and by John Braithwaite with Leah Dunn and Hilary Charlesworth in two subsequent trips to Bougainville and Port Moresby in 2007. Peacekeepers and other international players were also interviewed in the United States, Australia, New Zealand, Indonesia, the Solomon Islands, Fiji and Vanuatu between 2005 and 2010.

Our deepest thanks are to many Bougainvilleans and other Papua New Guineans on all sides of the conflict who generously gave their time and shared their insights, often on multiple occasions, in anonymous interviews. We thank the entire present and former staff of the Peace Foundation Melanesia, all of whom were particularly helpful in assisting us to meet key players, but special thanks to Clarence Dency and John Latu. Thanks also to the PNG Government, the Autonomous Bougainville Government, the Buka Open Campus of the University of Papua New Guinea (particularly Albert Nukuitu) and to the National Research Institute (particularly Jim Robins).

We benefited from participation in the wonderful Melanesian research community in Australia and at The Australian National University. Particular thanks to two of John Braithwaite's PhD students who worked on Bougainville theses, Kylie McKenna and Peter Reddy. We enjoyed many stimulating conversations with both of them. Peter is a co-author of this book because he participated in the first wave of data collection for a month in Bougainville, whereas Kylie was at an earlier stage of her work when the writing was substantially complete. We are grateful to Kylie for insights from her 2010 fieldwork in Bougainville, which was completed just before this book went to press.

Among our many generous colleagues, we single out Anthony Regan as a mentor to us throughout this research process. We were fortunate that all three of our major fieldwork trips overlapped with periods when Anthony was in Bougainville. Many were the evenings after our fieldwork when Anthony was able to correct what we thought were great insights acquired in the course of the day. He was also a gracious and wise colleague back in Canberra and an admirable contributor to the peace in Bougainville. Anthony's own most up-to-date contribution, *Light Intervention: Lessons from Bougainville*, will be published soon by the US Institute of Peace Press. We recommend it as the single most informative source on the past, present and future of the Bougainville peace process.

John Braithwaite and Hilary Charlesworth

The Australian National University

June 2010

Advisory Panel for the Bougainville case of Peacebuilding Compared

Dr Volker Boege, University of Queensland

Dr Bob Breen, The Australian National University

Anthony Regan, The Australian National University

Dr Ruth Saovana-Spriggs, The Australian National University

Professor Edward Wolfers, University of Wollongong

Glossary

ABG	Autonomous Bougainville Government
AusAID	Australian Agency for International Development
BCL	Bougainville Copper Limited
BIG	Bougainville Interim Government
BLF	Buka Liberation Front
BRA	Bougainville Revolutionary Army
BRF	Bougainville Resistance Forces
BTG	Bougainville Transitional Government
IMF	International Monetary Fund
NGO	non-governmental organisation
PMG	Peace Monitoring Group
PNG	Papua New Guinea
PNGDF	Papua New Guinea Defence Force
TMG	Truce Monitoring Group
UN	United Nations
UNDP	United Nations Development Programme
UNOMB	United Nations Observer Mission Bougainville
UNPOB	United Nations Political Office Bougainville

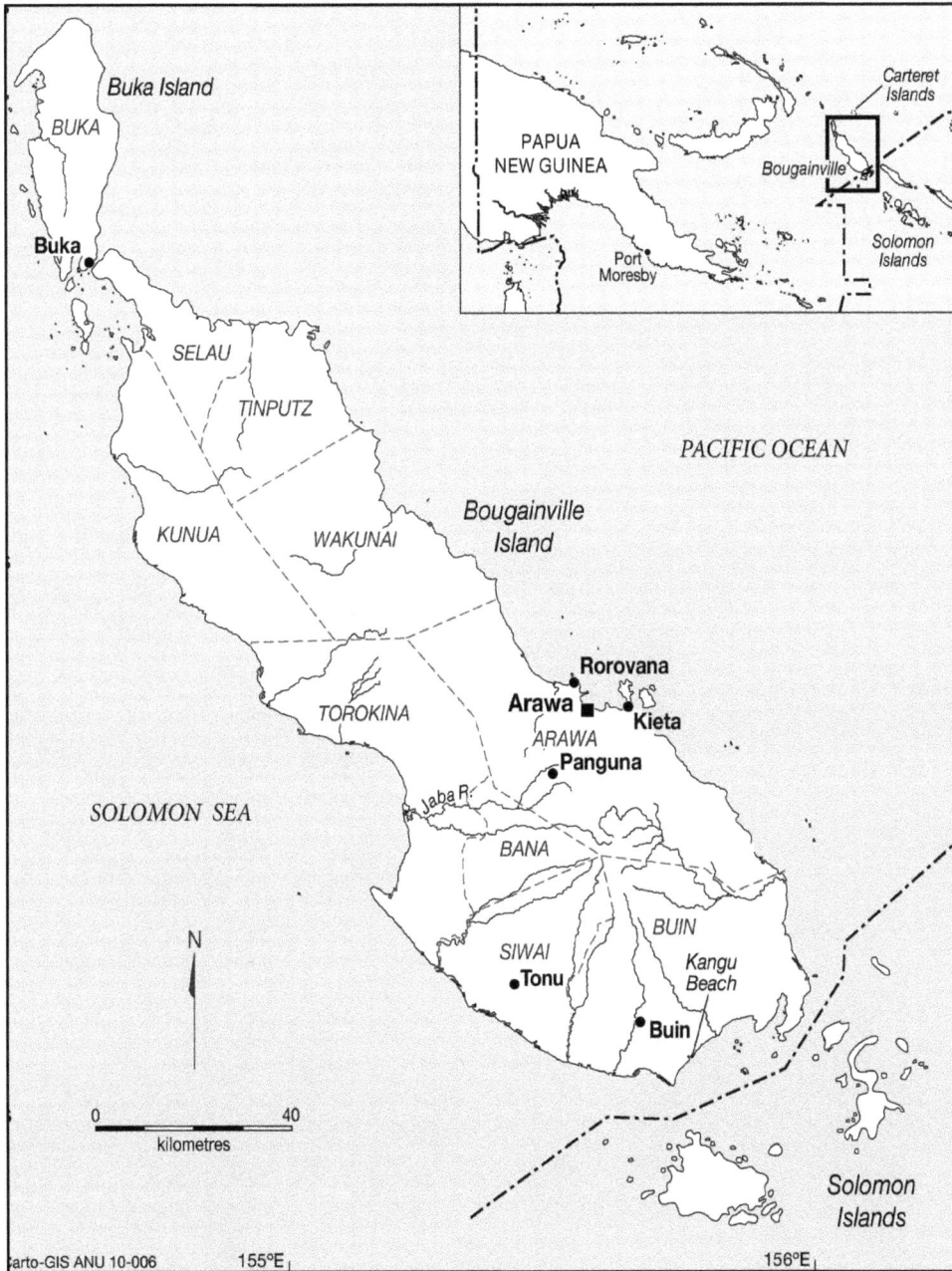

Map of Bougainville

1. Peacebuilding Compared and the Bougainville conflict

The story in brief

Bougainville suffered a terrible civil war for a decade from 1988 that pitted separatist forces of the Bougainville Revolutionary Army (BRA) against the national military and police of Papua New Guinea. The fighting evolved to set Bougainville factions against one another in the worst killing. This book argues that peacebuilding in Bougainville was shaped by bottom-up traditional and Christian reconciliation practices and a carefully crafted top-down political settlement. These two processes operated in symbiotic fashion, each making space for, and reinforcing, the other. There are important lessons in how each was designed and how one was connected to the other. For the student of peacebuilding, there is much to learn from the genius of this symbiosis between a top-down architecture of credible commitment and bottom-up reconciliation.

It has been a peace that has progressively become more resilient since 1998. The sequential sustaining of the peace has been patient—what Volker Boege (2006) has called a slow-food approach to peacebuilding. One wave of bottom-up reconciliation has built on previous waves, expanding the geographical reach of the peace and the breadth and depth of forgiveness across the society. The architecture of the top-down peace settlement has also been sequenced, with linkages that require one side to meet a commitment before the other side will deliver their next undertaking in an agreed sequence (Regan 2008; Wolfers 2006a). In this architecture, international peacekeepers played an exemplary role in securing the credible commitments. While peacekeepers were rarely hands-on mediators of the indigenous reconciliation, one of their greatest contributions was to initiate conversations between local enemies who were afraid of each other, allowing initial meetings to occur under the peacekeepers' security umbrella.

The conclusion of the book is that the very top-down architecture of the peace agreement that has been such a strength is also potentially its greatest weakness. This is because it is far from clear whether there is credible commitment of the PNG Parliament and of regional powers to the final crunch of the peace deal. If Bougainville votes in a referendum for independence in the course of this second decade of the twenty-first century—as provided for in the peace deal—and Papua New Guinea refuses to honour the wishes expressed in that vote, young men will be motivated to return to arms to vindicate the blood of their fathers. The sequence of credible commitments so honourably completed in the peace process to date could tragically heighten a sense of betrayal if the will of the people in the agreed referendum is dishonoured. Political leadership is needed in Port Moresby and regional preventive diplomacy is required to grasp the nettle of that final commitment. This can be delivered alongside an honourable and open political campaign to persuade the people of Bougainville that they could be better off if they vote for autonomous provincial government integrated within the state of Papua New Guinea.

In the next chapter, we place the conflict in the context of the colonial history, the history of mining exploitation and the identity politics of Bougainville. Subsequent chapters describe the unfolding of the violence itself and then of 11 peace processes that failed. The sequence of failed agreements nevertheless laid foundations for a final deal that has stuck for more than a decade. A fascinating feature of the final deal is that it was catalysed by a desperate attempt by Papua New Guinea's leadership to prevail militarily by contracting the private military corporation Sandline. When the international media, led by journalist Mary-Louise O'Callaghan, exposed the plan to deploy mercenaries, the plan collapsed, and ultimately Sandline collapsed.[1] As it raged, the Bougainville war seemed geopolitically obscure and more minor than it in fact was in scale. But in retrospect, many in the corridors of the United Nations see Bougainville as a success story of a sophisticated UN-backed peace architecture—a success that has reinvigorated the international norm against the use of mercenaries (Percy 2007) that was deeply endangered in the mid 1990s, and a peace that shows the potential of indigenous restorative justice in peacebuilding. The concluding two chapters of this book interpret more lessons from the conflict in comparative perspective.

---

1   Peace journalism is of neglected importance in the peacebuilding literature. In our first volume, we found peace journalism important in ending the major Indonesian conflicts of the past decade, and rumour-mongering, sensationalist journalism to be a contributor to the onset of some of those armed conflicts (Braithwaite et al. 2010). Mary-Louise O'Callaghan deserves to be honoured for breaking a story that revived the anti-mercenary norm internationally and connected Sandline in Bougainville to a wider politics of exposing the 'blood diamonds' trade in Africa and a nefarious mining company politics of interference in civil war through proxies such as Sandline. O'Callaghan was also an important player in our next volume on the Solomon Islands peace. A key Australian government strategic policymaker, Hugh White, tells the story of his old friend, Mary-Louise, calling him in 2000 to urge him to support a peacekeeping intervention in the Solomons. White recounts with some embarrassment, because he thinks it a pity in retrospect that O'Callaghan's advice was not followed at the time—his reply being that such a military intervention 'would not fit our paradigm' in the Pacific. O'Callaghan's retort, abruptly ending the conversation, was 'Well change your ****** paradigm'. Australia did change its paradigm, leading a regional peacekeeping intervention in the Solomon Islands in 2003 that so far has restored peace, with Hugh White a critical catalyst of the policy shift. During the intervening years, O'Callaghan had campaigned for that intervention in her columns in *The Australian* newspaper and other media.

The present chapter outlines the ambitions—methodological and substantive—of the Peacebuilding Compared project, of which this is the second volume. Readers who have read the first chapter of our first volume (Braithwaite et al. 2010) can skip to Chapter 2 without missing much.

Comparing conflict, comparing peacebuilding

The Peacebuilding Compared project adopts a broad conception of peacebuilding that is not distinguished from preventive diplomacy before conflict, peacemaking to end it or peacekeeping to monitor a peace agreement. Rather it is conceived here to incorporate all of these things, not wanting to separate peacebuilding after one conflict from preventive diplomacy to prevent a future one. Peacebuilding is therefore conceived here as tapping into a broad interpretation of peacebuilding as 'creation of a new environment' conducive to peace, in the words of former UN Secretary-General Boutros Boutros-Ghali (1995). The animating question for the project is what changes to an environment contribute most to enduring peace? We do not wish to close off by definition whether that contribution comes from this or that modality or phase of a peace process.

Peacebuilding Compared hopes over more than 20 years to code 670 variables in relation to the major armed conflicts that have raged across the world since 1990. The first large volume covered six different Indonesian armed conflicts (Braithwaite et al. 2010). It is hoped the third and fourth volumes will appear in quick succession to cover the Solomon Islands and then Timor-Leste. The project started with the region around the home country of the senior authors simply because it was easier to learn how to do it in the region with which the research team was most familiar.[2] As it happens, this region experienced a great deal of armed conflict during the 1990s. It was popularly referred to as 'the arc of instability' around Australia. As we enter the second decade of the twenty-first century, this arc is a much more stable, though vulnerable, region.

Peacebuilding Compared started in 2005. During the first five years of the project, the senior author managed to do some serious fieldwork across each of the sites in the four nations where these first 11 conflicts occurred.[3] In some

---

2 The senior author had dabbled at the beginning of the decade in some writing on peacebuilding in Indonesia after several trips there in the 1990s before and after the fall of President Suharto (Braithwaite 2002:Ch. 6), and spent time as an anthropology student living in a village in Bougainville at the end of the 1960s.

3 John Braithwaite was present for about 90 per cent of these interviews and he typed up the fieldwork notes or used voice-recognition software to record almost 90 per cent of them. The most common reason for not creating an electronic copy of fieldwork notes was that culpability for war crimes was discussed in the interview or other information was provided that might conceivably put someone in danger. The second most common reason was that there seemed so little that was truthful or valuable in them! Handwritten notes taken

cases, he was joined by co-authors for that case with far greater knowledge of that site and its languages. Joint is better, more reflexive and reliable than solitary fieldwork, but often is not logistically possible. Thankfully in the Bougainville case, most of the authors were able to spend many weeks together in the field with co-authors. We encourage a participatory approach to the research and invite readers to check out the Peacebuilding Compared web site at <http://peacebuilding.anu.edu.au>, where more information can be found. Please feel encouraged to post ideas and information to at any time throughout the 20-year life of the project.

For the project in general so far, we have been surprised by the level of access won to key players such as presidents, state and insurgent military commanders, foreign ministers, peace agreement negotiators and peacekeeping commanders. Yet, as is clear in the appendix to this volume, in comparison with the appendices in our first volume that summarised the types of players in the conflict who were interviewed, there was always uneven coverage in the types of stakeholders accessed. In every case, there were regional specialists in the study of this conflict who had secured broader access to the key players and who had talked many times to decision makers we did not mange to tap. This means it is always more important to attend to the published fruits of the fieldwork of others than to one's own fieldwork notes.

Yet this raises the question of what added value there could be in research of inferior coverage led by researchers with an inferior background in the regions of conflict. One added value is that sometimes inferior researchers whose fieldwork engagement is thin are nevertheless lucky enough to get superior access to some significant bits of information. So there is some value from our research in adding a little to the superior body of data and insights accumulated by the very best experts in these conflicts. Yet this is not the main contribution of comparative research. Its main added value is in the comparison and in the different ways of seeing that a comparative lens opens up. In each case study of Peacebuilding Compared, there tends to be a few scholars who have done the most insightful or thorough research on that case. The frequent citation of the work of these scholars makes it clear who they are. We are deeply grateful to them. Their work remains the scholarship to read on that case; but we do hope that by standing on their books, we might be able to peer over their shoulders to begin to see more clearly a comparative landscape of patterns of conflict across the globe.

---

during such interviews were still kept, in case a changed view of their truthfulness and value emerged later. No interviews were taped. Co-researchers had often done extensive fieldwork of their own for quite separate research projects—for example, associated with Peter Reddy's PhD thesis. The latter fieldwork is not included in the interview statistics summarised in the appendix at the end of this book.

Peacebuilding Compared offers a different kind of comparativism than the dominant kind that is based on quantitative analysis of statistical information from databases maintained by organisations such as the World Bank, the United Nations Development Programme (UNDP), the US Central Intelligence Agency and national statistics bureaus. Peacebuilding Compared uses these databases as well to code one-third of its 670 variables in relation to each conflict. Most codes, however, are of things not available in these databases, such as whether insurgents received training from a foreign power or whether significant numbers of the combatants were female, based on our interviews (and published fieldwork of others). Good examples of the kind of variable never coded in the leading quantitative research are the dynamics and shape of reconciliation processes post-conflict. This is a particularly important neglect according to some of the theoretical frameworks we address in this volume.

We also attempt to deal with two fundamental problems in the quantitative literature. One is that statisticians are often interested only in data coded at the national level. The study of 'civil wars' dominated by the disciplines of political science and international relations is often, moreover, interested only in armed conflicts in which one of the combatants is a state.[4] Peacebuilding Compared seeks to maximise coding at the local or provincial level. Hence the way a variable is coded for the separatist conflict in Aceh might be quite different from how it is coded for the separatist conflict in Papua at the other end of Indonesia. Another difference is that Peacebuilding Compared is content to code conflicts that are many things at once. For example, Peacebuilding Compared codes Aceh and Papua as both separatist and ethnic conflicts. This is different from the approach in the quantitative literature, which tends to force conflicts into one category or another. Third, as is clear from the summary in Table 9.1, we also enter certain codes as 'consensus' codes among scholars and other expert commentators on the case, and others as 'contested but credible'.

A difference from the ethnographic/qualitative literature is that Peacebuilding Compared is much less engaged with adjudicating the most contested debates about the case. We just code them as contested interpretations and we report the

---

4 Peacebuilding Compared studies armed conflicts in which one armed group with a command structure— even if its organisational auspices were episodic or non-institutionalised—engaged in group attacks with weapons on another armed group with a command structure. This means a clash of two warlord armies or two armed gangs can count as an armed conflict for Peacebuilding Compared if it passes certain other threshold conditions. For the moment, these are that two of the following three conditions are met: that at least 200 people were killed in the fighting within three years, at least 30 000 people were driven from their homes by the fighting and an internationally sanctioned peacekeeping mission was sent to make peace in the war-torn region. Including the last condition prevents us from excluding from consideration serious armed conflicts that started but were prevented from escalating into mass slaughter by peacekeepers (for example, the arrival of UN peacekeepers in Timor-Leste in 2006). This, however, is just a starting definition for our armed conflicts that could change as new wars occur. It sets a threshold that excludes a lot of conflicts that one might want to include. Bougainville is a civil war that clearly exceeds all three provisional thresholds we have set for inclusion.

nature of the contestation in our narrative. What we are interested in doing is ruling out non-credible interpretations. Conflict zones are teeming with them: wild unsubstantiated rumours, ridiculous theories propagated by people who spread lies to protect their culpability, clever pieces of misinformation planted by double agents, imagined histories concocted by supposed combatants with grandiose visions of their self-importance to saving their nation. A significant level of fieldwork on the ground and in the capitals of combatant and peacekeeping states (or at UN headquarters) is needed. The intent is not to get the research team to the point where it can settle the most contested debates among the experts, but to the point where it can rule out most (hopefully all) the myriad non-credible interpretations.

A distinctive comparativism

This renders Peacebuilding Compared a distinctive form of comparativism. The approach was motivated by reading most of the best research as falling into one of two camps. The first includes a large number of wonderful studies of particular conflicts—or comparing a couple—written by scholars who have deep knowledge and long experience of that region. The second is the more recent quantitative tradition led by outstanding comparativists such as Ted Gurr, Jack Goldstone, Paul Collier, Anke Hoeffler, Virginia Page Fortna, James Fearon, David Laitin, Michael Doyle and Nicholas Sambanis, among others cited in the references. In choosing a method that aspires to significant fieldwork engagement that is inferior to the best ethnographic work, and is on a smaller number of cases than the best quantitative work, we are simply filling a methodological niche that has been under-exploited in the literature. We do not have the view that it is necessarily a superior method to the dominant two.[5]

---

5   One battleground between large-n quantitative methods and single case studies arises from the qualitative critique that quantitative methods freeze (into one code) dynamic phenomena that are one thing at one point in time, another thing at another point in an unfolding conflict. This means that case studies of single conflicts do not in fact have an n of 1. Rather, they are studies of many separate episodes of violence, some of which might be more ethnic, others more religious or involving attacks by different ethnic groups than the first episode. Hence, combining the results of X qualitative analyses of protracted conflicts is more like a qualitative meta-analysis than it is like combining X cases each with an n of 1. What we are attempting in Peacebuilding Compared is a unique kind of meta-analytical hybrid. John Braithwaite deploys his knowledge of the narratives of the set of episodes of violence that makes up a particular case to code most variables as 'high', 'average' or 'low' on that variable. If there is some doubt about how to code (a common occurrence), it is coded 'average'. So, 'average' is given the broad meaning of 'the range on this variable where most cases of armed conflict in Peacebuilding Compared lie'. If there is both doubt and thinness of data that make it very hard to code, it is also coded as 'hard to code'. Imagine coding two variables on the extent to which greed and grievance are motivations for fighting. The first point to make is that they can both be high or both low, or they can have different values. The second is that if greed is highly prominent in some episodes, moderately present in most and totally absent in some, the greed variable will be coded 'average'. So these three-point codes are in fact crude summaries from a sometimes large number of data points within the single case. For some variables, such as the number of combatants on various sides and the number of refugees, we code a real number (or estimate a midpoint of a best-guess range). But we code both a maximum number (the

One of its demands is that it requires one person to read very extensively on each case and to be in the room or under the tree for most of the fieldwork. Otherwise it would be impossible to code the 670 variables consistently across cases. Otherwise the thematic unity of narrative volumes such as this might offer no advance on an edited collection of haphazard comparisons—insightful though such casual comparativism can be.

By 2030, we hope that some sort of cluster analysis or fuzzy set analysis to the best quantitative standards of that time will reveal something new about types of conflicts. We would also hope to define which might be the most important of probably a long list of risk factors that conduce to the persistence of armed conflict—and which are the most important protective factors for preserving peace. Narrative and analytical books such as this lay an important foundation for this future quantitative work. They discover new variables that are worth coding for all cases and new complexities in the dynamics among these variables that might ultimately account for why certain quantitative models will not explain much and why others might do so.

A final part of the method was to invite the people who seemed to be producing some of the best insights and writing the best books on the case to be members of an advisory panel. Our thanks to Sinclair Dinnen for this idea. We asked the advisory panel to suggest important people to interview, to read our first draft, comment on erroneous insights within it and on research and lines of inquiry that needed to be pursued before the next draft. Many were internationally distinguished scholars. Others were PhD students, including a number from The Australian National University, who had the luxury of recently spending long periods in the field, which senior scholars sometimes cannot manage.

Our ethical obligations under The Australian National University's Research Ethics Committee approval were explained to all participants. These included an obligation to report quotes and insights from each informant without identifying them unless they specifically indicated that they wanted to be quoted as the source of an insight. Wherever a quote appears without a citation to some other source in the literature, it is an anonymous quote from an informant interviewed for Peacebuilding Compared.

---

high-water mark of the number of combatants or refugees across all episodes of the conflict) and a separate variable, which is an estimated average number across the various episodes of the conflict. All this is perhaps only slightly less crude than a purported single quantitative estimate for a single conflict (as in the extant quantitative literature). However crude, it is an attempt to quantitatively summarise from qualitative cases that are more than narratives of an n of 1. This is exemplified by the discussion in the last two pages of Chapter 9 of why there are 12 data points in the Bougainville history relevant to confirming Barbara Walter's (2002) hypothesis that reciprocity in step-by-step demobilisation is needed for peace. Moreover, this approach to aggregating from a multiple-n sensibility for each conflict is combined with actually writing an episodic, dynamic narrative for that conflict. This is what we are doing in this book. The hope is that new kinds of insights will ultimately come from the interplay between multiple case-study narratives and quantitative analysis of the codes with this multiple-n sensibility.

2. Historical background to the conflict

Papua New Guinea is a nation of six million people that has regional geopolitical significance, sharing a long border with Indonesia. Bougainville is a large island (surrounded by smaller islands, the largest of which is Buka separated by a narrow strait from Bougainville Island) north-east of the island of New Guinea and north-west of the Solomon Islands. Ferocious fighting between Japanese and Australian and US forces took place in Bougainville during World War II. This resulted in a decline of the indigenous population of perhaps 25 per cent, the flight of Europeans and Chinese from Bougainville and cost the lives of 42 000 foreign soldiers (Nelson 2005:194–6). Papua New Guinea gained independence from its Australian colonial masters in 1975. In the years before independence, there had been agitation for Bougainville not to become part of Papua New Guinea. Most people of Bougainville saw themselves (with the blackest skin in the Pacific) connected racially, culturally and by historical trading relationships much more with the Solomon Islands than with Papua New Guinea. Over time, an independent nation of Bougainville, rather than integration with the Solomon Islands, became a rallying cause. A civil war that for many was aimed at independence broke out in 1988, continuing to 1997. After years of negotiations, in 2005 an Autonomous Bougainville Government (ABG) was established within Papua New Guinea.

International support for Bougainville's independence was almost non-existent. The general reaction was that Papua New Guinea was struggling to be viable as a nation, so what chance would an island of 160 000 people (just before the war) have? Today the population is probably more than 200 000. Bougainvilleans themselves looked around and saw a Pacific of island micro-states separated from other island states by vast expanses of ocean. Like most of them, Bougainville was diverse, with Polynesian enclaves as well as the dominant Melanesian population. Sixteen Austronesian and nine non-Austronesian (Papuan) languages are spoken on Bougainville (Tryon 2005).

Early history

We know humans have occupied Bougainville for more than 29 000 years (Spriggs 2005), but we know little about the dates of their arrival and from where they travelled. There were extensive trading relationships with islands to the north and south. The southern trade with what are now the Solomon Islands imported shell money (which was ceremonially central in Bougainville), lime and fish in exchange for pigs, vegetables, pottery and decorated weapons (Oliver 1973:20).

Europeans first paid attention to the large island when two French ships commanded by Louis de Bougainville anchored there in 1768. Between 1820 and 1860, British, French and American whaling vessels became more frequent visitors and took on some Bougainvillean crew. After 1870, large numbers of Bougainvilleans were forced or volunteered to work as indentured labourers on plantations in Queensland, Fiji, Samoa and New Britain (Oliver 1973:23). In 1902, the Catholic Society of Mary (the Marists) established a mission on Bougainville. From the 1880s, the territories later to form Papua New Guinea were administered by Britain (then from 1906, Australia) and Germany. The German Colonial Administration in Rabaul annexed Bougainville in 1884 and opened a post at Kieta in 1905. Germany and Britain agreed to split the Solomon Islands, with the most northerly islands (mainly Bougainville Island) going to Germany. A few European planters and traders began to settle on the coast about the turn of the twentieth century. Before 1905, the most commercially important German copra plantation firm, the Neuguinea-Kompagnie, provided the nearest thing to an administration in Bougainville. German rule ended in 1914 when an Australian expeditionary force arrived. After World War I, the League of Nations granted Australia a mandate to govern the German territory in New Guinea, including Bougainville, and after World War II the entire territory became part of the United Nations' international trusteeship system, administered by Australia until independence in 1975.

The Europeans found societies that lived well off the land, growing taro,[1] green vegetables, tropical fruits, coconut, breadfruit, almonds and sago, fishing and eating occasional meat from pigs and possum. Large villages of hundreds of people were common on the coast. Most Bougainvilleans, however, lived in multi-household hamlets of a grandmother's family, her daughters' families and her granddaughters' families. Each household comprised a husband and a wife or wives and their children. Marriage did not occur within a matrilineage, so men would move to live in another matrilineal hamlet on marriage. Cultural exceptions are Buin, Siwai, Nissan Island and the outlying Polynesian Islands, which are patrilineal (Saovana-Spriggs 2007:8). Among the matrilineal Nasioi, marriages do occur within the same clan (Ogan 1972:14). While cultural differences across Bougainville are considerable, across the whole island similar clans recur, often with the same totem and origin myth of the clan.[2] People can therefore travel to unfamiliar parts of the island and experience some sense of

---

1   Shifting to sweet potato after World War II.
2   In some places, clans are divided into two exogamous moieties.

spiritual and ritual unity with others from their clan who live there. I can ask for and receive help from people of my clan whom I have never met and who do not speak my language. The Catholic Church, and to a lesser extent smaller Protestant churches, has become another unifying spiritual influence. A final integrative force spread by the Catholic education system, but initiated by the indentured labour system for plantation production by workers from different language groups, was the gradual spread of Tok Pisin (Pidgin), which is now the lingua franca.

Groups of residential hamlets formed fighting units of variable composition depending on male leadership contingencies. In some regions (Buin, Buka, some of North Bougainville), leadership is hereditary, but mostly it is based on feats of leadership such as giving feasts for large aggregations of people. Warfare seems to have been common across Bougainville in pre-European times (Oliver 1973:72)—though see Oliver's (1955:412–18) own doubts based on interviews with older men on how many battles they had in fact experienced. In Buka and the far north of Bougainville, victors engaged in cannibalism, while headhunting was common in the south. Warfare was, however, regulated by sophisticated peacemaking practices, such that while warfare was frequent, loss of life was almost always modest. One reason why there is so much to learn from peacebuilding in Bougainville is that Bougainvilleans have such vast cultural experience as brokers of war and brokers of peace. The Catholic Church led a process of religiously justified pacification that was effective in ending intertribal warfare and wiping out cannibalism and headhunting. When anthropology student John Braithwaite spoke to old men who had eaten human flesh in Bougainville in 1969, they spoke with a certain shame of practices that predated their enlightenment by the word of God. Pacification also depended on the German and then Australian colonial authorities demonstrating superior firepower. This was accomplished by very small numbers of colonial police training and arming local 'police boys'. It is impossible to say how much of the credit for pacification rests with these guns or with the sermons of the missionaries or with deaths from European diseases. But as has been conjectured with Dutch pacification in Eastern Indonesia, Howley (2002:22) notes that pacification occurred so quickly and easily in Bougainville that both the Bible and the gun could have been little more than excuses for indigenous peacemakers to grasp a permanent peace with their neighbours that they had long wanted.

Pacification also proceeded through indirect rule by coopting big-men—respected leaders renowned for giving large feasts—and appointing them as *luluai* (the word for chief in one New Britain language). These men were given a badge, hat and silver-headed stick and could retain 10 per cent of the colonial taxes they collected. The essentials of the *luluai* (renamed *kukerai* or hatmen after their police hats) system were retained under Australian colonialism. For much of Australian colonial history in Bougainville, the province was ruled indirectly by just four very junior subdistrict *kiaps*.

As talk of independence for Papua New Guinea began to get serious in the 1960s, there were leaders in Bougainville who wanted to go it alone, or with the Solomon Islands. Great impetus was given to this movement by the discovery of mineral wealth, which secessionists believed might underwrite independence, but particularly by the way the mine was established—as discussed in the next section. In 1968, a group of Bougainvillean students, civil servants and politicians living in Port Moresby formed the Mungkas (a Buin word for black) Society. It became a crucible of secessionist thought and activism. Back in central Bougainville in 1969, a secessionist social movement, Napidakoe Navitu, quickly gained a large following.

The mine

In 1964, a huge copper and gold deposit was discovered near the centre of Bougainville. By the standards of the time, Bougainville Copper Limited (BCL), whose principal investor was Conzinc Riotinto Australia (CRA), had a comparatively advanced sense of corporate social responsibility. This was based on an enlightened self-interest whereby management advised shareholders that unless they treated the emerging nation of Papua New Guinea and its citizens well through the economic opportunities it created, a future leadership of the independent nation might nationalise such a large asset. BCL funded tertiary scholarships for indigenous students without requiring eventual company employment. It funded agricultural extension. It provided capital for Bougainvillean business start-ups through the Panguna Development Foundation. BCL agreed with government demands that it, rather than the government, pay for nearly all the infrastructure the mine needed: roads, electricity, water, telecommunications, ports, airstrips, housing.

The PNG Territory Administration exercised an option to acquire 20 per cent of the equity in the mine and also received a royalty of 1.25 per cent on the value of its revenue from copper-concentrate sales for the 42-year term of the lease. A large number of shares were reserved for purchase by indigenous individuals and groups and many were purchased by church organisations, for example, though we do not know how many individual Bougainvilleans benefited. There were, however, 9000 PNG resident shareholders (Griffin 2005:295). The company agreed to comparatively high territorial taxes on its profits, starting with a three-year tax holiday (terminated 15 months early), then a 50 per cent company tax rate (rather than the normal 25 per cent [Regan 2003]), increasing over the years to a maximum rate of 66 per cent (Oliver 1973:158). Michael Somare's PNG coalition government in 1974 responded to criticism that the mine was exploitative by renegotiating upwards the government's share of earnings. We will see that by contemporary standards, the BCL deal was a very good one for the PNG state, but miserly to local landowners. It was the offer to local landowners that was a major proximate cause of the war.

A deal struck the year the Bougainville war started granted landowners in Porgera more than 20 times the share in the earnings of the mine in royalties compared with what the Panguna landowners received (Matthew 2000:736). This was part of a general shift among mining companies in Papua New Guinea and beyond as a result of what were seen as the mistakes of Bougainville 'from paying resource rents to the state for technocratic distribution in the national interest towards paying resource rents to landowners in the immediate vicinity of their operations' (Claxton 1998:96). Claxton (1998:97) goes on to criticise this strategy as 'hastening the retreat or even capitulation of the state before the power of multinational companies and local interests'. Anthony Regan pointed out in commenting on this paragraph that the same sort of deal was indeed being offered in Bougainville that year.

PNG leader Somare also in 1974 sought to counter the growing threat of Bougainville secession by negotiations that led to an Interim Provincial Government and by passing all the royalties from the mine (as opposed to the larger tax revenues) through to the province (apart from the 5 per cent of the 1.25 per cent royalty that went to landowners). In September 1975, the Interim Provincial Government of Bougainville nevertheless declared independence unilaterally. The PNG National Parliament suspended it the next month and anti-PNG Government riots ensued in Bougainville. During 1976, Somare settled this conflict by agreeing to a permanent provincial government with some credible powers and resources: the North Solomon Islands Provincial Government. There were also undertakings to further devolve powers to the province over time, though these were mostly not honoured (Momis 2005:315).

The mine was a massive, complex operation in exceptionally rugged terrain that required a great deal of expatriate engineering and mining expertise. Nevertheless, the company had a commitment to create indigenous employment and to train locals to take over from expatriates. At the peak of construction in 1971—much of it by non-BCL employees—there were 3861 expatriate and 6328 PNG employees.[3] There were basic problems with BCL's corporate responsibility analysis. Its enlightened self-interest was driven by fear of expropriation by Port

---

3   This fell to a workforce of about 4000 for much of the 1980s, about one-third of whom were Bougainvillean. Another 4000—about half Bougainvillean—were employed in businesses dependent on BCL (Joint Standing Committee on Foreign Affairs, Defence and Trade 2005:18).

Moresby politicians or by what Anthony Regan called a PNG administrative state characterised by limited mobilisation around political identities until the approach of independence, so BCL royalties, taxes and reserved shares were designed mainly to impress elites in the capital and its affirmative-action policies measured success in creating employment opportunities for citizens of all Papua New Guinea. This is not to say it did not also try hard to create opportunities for Bougainvilleans; about half the apprentices and half of the highest paid Papua New Guineans were local Nasioi.[4] Its success in creating opportunities for imported workers—especially from the New Guinea Highlands—was, however, one of the factors that led to civil war. Second, BCL's corporate responsibility analysis—in a manner typical in the 1960s—was focused on creating economic opportunities for a poor nation to the neglect of environmental impacts. The colonial administration also embedded dysfunctional regulatory arrangements in the Bougainville Copper Agreement such that the PNG Minister for the Environment in 1988 could complain that his department was prevented from taking action against pollution by the mine because the agreement vested that authority in the Department of Minerals and Energy (Gillespie 1999:13). BCL was probably a comparatively environmentally concerned miner for its time, yet the environmental impacts turned out to be huge. And their effects were concentrated on large communities around Panguna and in the river valleys between the mine and the coast. Within these deeply aggrieved communities— indeed communities that were grieving for their lands—the conflict began. The mine was a large physical scar on the land, but a deeper spiritual one for communities whose landscape was intensely implicated in their spiritual life.

Most fundamentally, BCL's attempts to be a responsible corporate citizen were to no avail simply because the mine was so big—far bigger than any mine in Australia. Some 150 000 tonnes of rock waste and tailings were discharged every day from the mine area (Brown 1974:19). It could not be dug without formidable displacement of villages and displacement of soil that washed down steep mountain valleys into rivers that became dead zones. It could not be built without thousands of men with white and brown skin (or 'redskins', as the locals called the New Guineans) who could not but dominate the local space, who consumed too much alcohol, harassed local women and created a deep sense of dread that the local culture, laws and identity were being crushed. The outside workers also brought problems of public drunkenness and prostitution that were new to the area and scandalised church elders. Paul Lapun put it this way in 1988: 'You didn't tell me what would happen to my environment…

---

4   But in 1971 the total of Nasioi BCL employees was only 241 (Denoon 2000:168). So while BCL was trying to husband the best skill-development opportunities for Nasioi, most of the 20 000 Nasioi did not get jobs in the mine and there was still a feeling of having their land overwhelmed by massive numbers of immigrant workers in Panguna and Arawa. Nasioi people were more unskilled in vocational terms than people from many other parts of Papua New Guinea.

When I was young they fooled me and now I am old and still alive to see the result of my decision I weep. Who cares for a copper mine if it kills us' (Denoon 2000:200).

These grievances also created opportunities for locals motivated by greed. Some we interviewed thought the founder of the BRA, Francis Ona, was one of those men. Most considered he was not, but that there were others who promoted the war to advance interests in controlling the mine, controlling Bougainville, capturing the Panguna Landowners' Association, and so on. So the sheer size of the physical and economic impacts of the mine made for both huge grievances and huge opportunities for greed.

BCL got off to a bad start by prospecting the land without the permission of landowners and with some unsophisticated and offensive analysis to the effect that the Panguna Valley was uninhabited and sparsely utilised. There was incompetence in failing to come to grips with the complexities of shared tenure for land and a crude imposition of colonial land and mining laws over the top of this complexity. There was a failure to grasp the spiritual, cultural and social dimensions of land; it was not simply the commodity that BCL negotiators treated it as being. Minister for Territories, Charles (Ceb) Barnes, was not listening when he visited Bougainville in 1969. His interpreter told us that women from the mine site sang a song for Barnes about how sacred the land was for them and about their incomprehension of why it was being taken away: 'In matrilineal society, when women wail and confront something, it's a big signal.' Barnes did not hear it and rambled about the nation's minerals belonging to the whole nation.

Some of the brightest and best Australian lawyers of that generation—Anthony Mason advising the Commonwealth as Solicitor-General and Ninian Stephen as counsel for BCL—were offering advice on how to fend off any Australian High Court challenge that might enforce a more sensitive engagement with the indigenous land-tenure issues. Ultimately, the High Court did hear the matter and decided in 1969 that Australia had the power to take land in Commonwealth territories without the obligations to provide just compensation (*Teori Tau vs The Commonwealth*, [1969] CLR 564; Havini 1999:8). Beneath all of that failure to come to grips with the complexity of the land BCL devastated, there was a simple conflict that was more irresolvable between the principle of the national development of a poor nation and a pre-modern, local understanding of shared ownership: 'The principle that royalties paid on the treasure from one's own land would be used for the Territory as a whole, and not for the land's owners, or even for Bougainvilleans in general, was considered by some Bougainvilleans to be insanely alien, or transparently deceitful' (Oliver 1973:164).

Bougainville's House of Assembly member, Paul Lapun, struggled for years to eventually rally colleagues from across Papua New Guinea to roll the colonial administration and allocate 5 per cent of the 1.25 per cent copper royalty to the Panguna landowners. Sadly, though, fighting over that modest pot became another factor contributing to the conflict. Because the politics of land rights had delayed a lucrative flow of profits, when distributions to local landowners began, there was 'more haste than planning' (Denoon 2000:169). Crude, inaccurate procedures were implemented for calculating who was entitled to what share; 'the view from Canberra overlooked such difficulties' (Denoon 2000:169). The interest in Canberra was in announcements of the aggregate dollars paid out to indigenes. These dollar amounts were unprecedented in the Pacific and sounded impressive, but they were in fact little compensation for removing the homes, the lands, the livelihoods, the spiritual lives and the entire way of life of people.

Resistance to the mine became a major regional news story in 1969 when Australian media covered the physical resistance of women and men in Rorovana, where BCL built a port for the mine. The footage was shocking: bare-breasted women putting their bodies in the path of Australian bulldozers, resisting passively and being attacked by helmeted riot police with batons. The newspaper headlines—'Australia's shame', 'Australia's bullies' (Denoon 2000:2)—did indeed outrage many Australians. They added to the impetus in the Australian labour movement to push for early independence for Papua New Guinea. The international coverage did raise some questions of how different the meaning of land was to Bougainvilleans compared with white Australians. Three young Bougainvilleans—one of them Theodore Miriung, who in 1996 was to be assassinated as Premier of the Bougainville Transitional Government— said 'land is our physical life—food and sustenance. Land is our social life; it is marriage; it is status; it is politics; in fact, it is our only world' (Dove et al. 1974:29). Donald Denoon's (2000:127) account of why the story had little traction beyond the South Pacific is revealing, as in the words of one agency journalist, 'the violence itself was quite a good little spot news story but the real story about background and motives is too complicated for overseas readers, it would take too long to explain'.

The Rorovana incidents sent a warning signal that should have triggered more nuanced analysis towards preventive diplomacy by the social democrats Gough Whitlam[5] and Michael Somare, who were surging relentlessly towards leadership of their nations. Whitlam and Somare—like the conservative

---

5 Edward Wolfers made the interesting comment on our draft that 'Gough Whitlam, in particular, was always clear that the decision for Papua New Guinea's independence was at least as much concerned with the future of Australia (Australia's international reputation, and the effects that continued colonial rule might have on Australian society) as of Papua New Guinea.'

minister Barnes,[6] the senior bureaucrats in Port Moresby and the leadership of BCL—proved incapable of preventing the war by re-examining the social justice of the mine through the lens of the local landowners. Having BCL contribute even more to the national development of Papua New Guinea seemed to them all the appropriate social democratic paradigm of responsiveness required.[7] Investigative journalists and university experts did not excel at analysing and communicating to political, business and administrative elites the complexity of the responsiveness that was needed. Instead of constructive international engagement with preventive diplomacy, the Rorovana warning signal simply produced self-righteous vilification of an exploitative multinational, of overzealous policing and of a callous colonial administration. Independence for Papua New Guinea and tougher rents and taxation of BCL would fix that in the eyes of an Australian democratic left that was at its zenith of community support as the opening of the mine approached.

BCL was getting much more sophisticated advice from a fine anthropologist in Douglas Oliver of Harvard University. While Oliver saw many of the flaws in the way BCL was managing the land-compensation issues, and spoke out against them, he did not allow these to shake his ultimate advice that 'opposition would be limited, and that people would be reconciled to the mine eventually' (Denoon 2000:201). Social science is useful in diagnosing the problems a particular course of action might cause and even in making probabilistic predictions of what is more and less likely across a large n of cases. It is not useful for predicting what will happen in an n of 1. Douglas Oliver made an n-of-1 prediction in the section of his 1968 report to CRA headed 'Some predictions regarding external relations between CRA and Bougainville natives' (Denoon 2000:217). This rosy 'it will blow over' analysis was one of the obstacles to the preventive diplomacy needed to head off the war.

In 1978, landowners became more organised, uniting to form the Panguna Landowners' Association to lobby over their many grievances. BCL hoped the landowners would give up if it kept delaying and fobbing them off; however, BCL negotiated a new compensation package supplementary to the major agreement with the PNG Government after frustrated landowners looted the Panguna supermarket. This established a Road Mine Tailings Leases Trust Fund that invested in local plantations and in the Panguna Development Foundation. The new fund was designed to provide some basic services to landowners in education, health care, water supply, transportation and scholarships for

---

6   The senior author had conversations with Whitlam and his successor as Labor leader, Bill Hayden, in Bougainville when they visited in 1969. He also ineffectively raised concerns with Ceb Barnes in this period in the context of helping set up public meetings in which Barnes and Hayden spoke on the mine.

7   Anthony Regan, in commenting on this paragraph, added that Bougainvillean political leaders in the 1970s were focused more on securing limited resources from the mine revenue for their new Interim Provincial Government than on securing substantial redistribution to landowners.

students in higher education (Okole 1990). Many landowners, however, came to view the fund as operating for the personal gain of board members of the Panguna Landowners' Association.

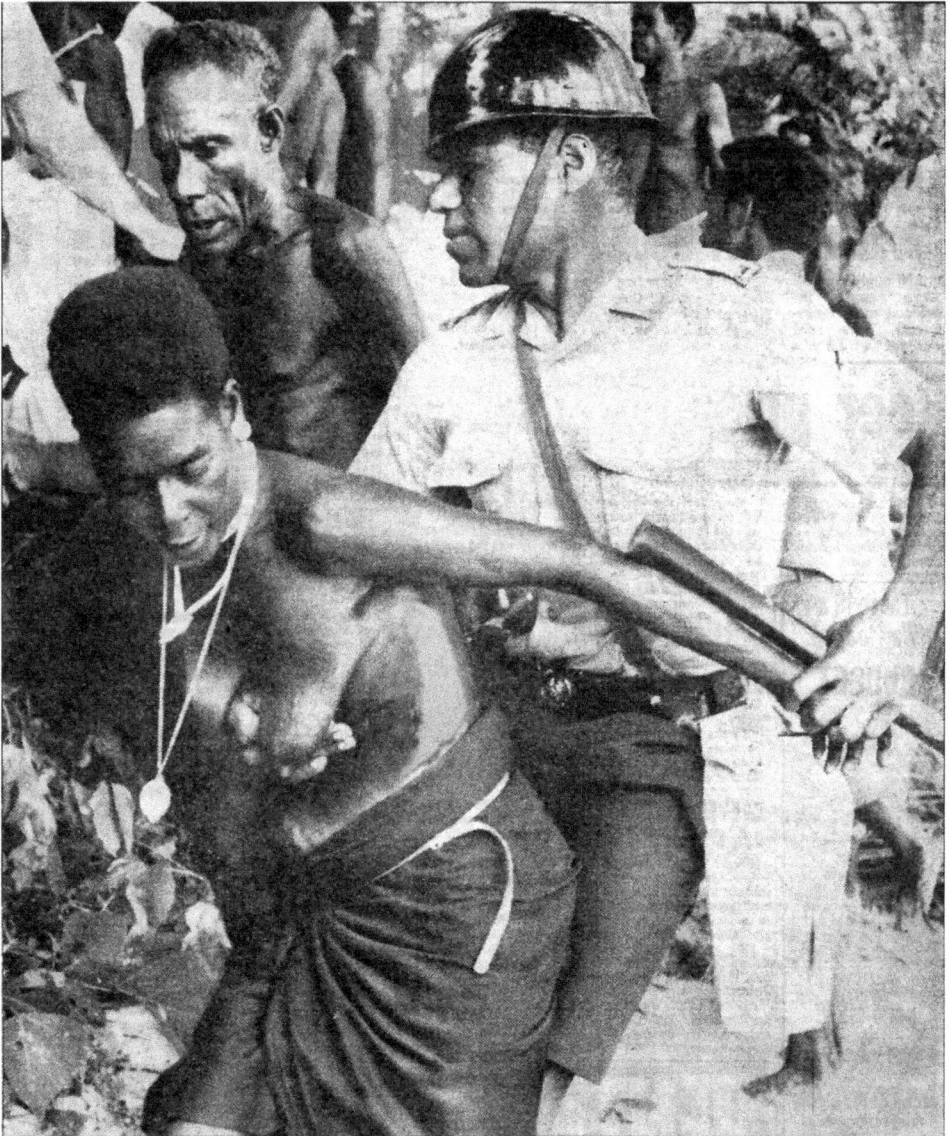

Figure 2.1 Rorovana women resist the bulldozers moving in, 6 August 1969

Photo: *Sydney Sun*

A combination of infighting among Bougainvillean political leaders who were on guard against adversaries gaining credit for getting a better deal for landowners (Griffin 1990:11) and a recession that was pinching BCL and PNG Government finances meant that the 1981 review of the mining agreement (provided for in

Somare's 1974 renegotiation) never occurred. This did not help the legitimacy of the Panguna Landowners' Association. '[H]ad the government under Prime Minister Sir Julius Chan renegotiated the BCA [Bougainville Copper Agreement] in 1981, the bloody Bougainville crisis may have been pre-empted' (Momis 2005:310).

A new generation frustrated by not only BCL but the non-confrontational politics of their elders, led by Francis Ona and Perpetua Serero,[8] formed the New Panguna Landowners' Association in 1987. Melchior Togolo (2005:285) and some whom we interviewed alleged that greed was a motive, that some in the new association were 'refused loans because of past loan delinquency' after more rigorous accountability for its trust fund was introduced. What they demanded was massive and they were not taken seriously: K10 billion for environmental damage, 50 per cent of BCL profits and transfer of BCL to Bougainvillean ownership within five years. Carruthers' (1990:41) summary of the relative share of wealth generated by the mine from 1972 to 1989 shows how unrealistic the K10 billion plus 50 per cent of profits claim was and how little of the wealth from the mine went to Bougainville—particularly the landowners:

- K million
- National government 1078
- Provincial government 75
- Landholders 24
- Non-government shareholders 577
- Total 1754

Carruthers' numbers above also show that the national and provincial governments were making (in taxes, fees and dividends) twice as much from the mine as the mostly foreign private shareholders.[9] These numbers are about the share of profits in the wealth created by the mine. There is also labour's share—a large proportion of which went to citizens of Papua New Guinea. While the minority expatriate employees were much more highly paid, they spent a lot of their salaries in Papua New Guinea.

In August 1988, the New Panguna Landowners' Association occupied the offices of the foundation controlled by the association and declared the appointment of a new board of the association. A key member of the old board, Mathew Kove, was allegedly murdered on the orders of his nephew, Francis Ona, in early 1989. By then, the legal battle over control of the association was moot as the mine was about to close and the New Panguna Landowners' Association had launched the BRA as a Bougainville-wide uprising led by Ona.

---

8   Perpetua Serero died soon after the civil war began.
9   Similar proportions apply in the numbers provided in a more detailed breakdown by Hilson (2007:29).

Closure of the mine in May 1989 because of the violence was a massive setback for the PNG economy. The mine was providing 45 per cent of Papua New Guinea's export income, 17 per cent of internally generated government revenue and 12 per cent of gross domestic product (GDP) (Carruthers 1990:38). It had completed 1000 apprenticeships and trained 11 000 PNG employees in industrial skills, which many had taken to jobs in other parts of the economy. Four hundred tertiary graduations had been funded. All this training input into the PNG and Bougainville economies stopped with the war.

Immigration

Concern was widespread in the areas where immigrant workers were employed (by BCL and its contractors and also as plantation workers) over disrespect for local customs and local women, especially by Highlanders from New Guinea. Highlanders were seen as primitive, especially because of their quick propensity for payback violence. An incident in the Highlands in 1972 focused this stereotype. Two respected Bougainvillean civil servants—one a physician— were beaten to death after they struck and killed a little girl with their car. Some research at the time among southern Bougainville students ranked a hierarchy of social acceptance that placed 'New Guineans' highest (after Bougainvilleans), followed by 'Papuans', 'Europeans' and, last, 'Highlanders' (Nash and Ogan 1990:10; Moulik 1977:103–6).

Immigrant workers from the mainland established many squatter settlements in Central Bougainville, some of which became violence hotspots or were perceived that way. The conditions of dislocation created by rapid urban development in fact also incubated a great deal of violence and property crime by Bougainvillean gangs. In addition to taking thousands of jobs at the mine, the migrants bought up many local businesses such as bus services. Howley (2002:33) alleges that mainlanders ran three brothels. Another 'redskin' ran an organised crime business based on gang members robbing houses. These were disturbing developments for the formerly well-ordered, low-crime Bougainvillean societies.

The rape, murder and mutilation of a popular nurse from the hospital unleashed a fury against 'redskins' in 1988. The 'Koromira Home Guard' armed and cleared their area of 'redskins', killing any men who resisted (Howley 2002:35).

Conclusion

There was a historical basis and a movement for Bougainville separatism before the mine. We will see in the next chapter that when dissatisfaction over the mine and over the related issue of immigration boiled over as violence, Francis Ona was able to broaden his armed coalition by linking the mine issue and the immigration issue to the separatist movement. The Australian left and progressive forces within BCL itself were concerned about the mine causing injustice—or being seen by Papua New Guinea to cause it—from the late 1960s. But they viewed this injustice in the frame of a wealthy multinational exploiting a Third-World nation. Their emphasis was therefore on compensating the PNG Government for environmental destruction and guaranteeing Port Moresby a generous windfall from the profits. This involved a misunderstanding of the more local nature of the felt injustice that would endanger peace and development. Both BCL and its critics on the left in Australia failed in particular to grasp the importance of clumsy compensation policies that opened divisions between old and young local landowners and between landowners and 'redskin' immigrant workers.

3. Descent into civil war

Major fighting begins

In 1987 and 1988, the New Panguna Landowners' Association organised public demonstrations, some of which culminated in attacks on BCL property. The landowners were joined in their attacks on mine property by some young mine workers who felt discriminated against as Bougainvilleans by BCL. November 1988 saw a decisive escalation from minor looting and arson to the use of explosives to blow up BCL electrical pylons along the Panguna Highway and destroy property at the mine site. We might call the demolition of the pylons and the vigorous reaction of the PNG security forces to it as the triggers for the formation of the Bougainville Revolutionary Army (BRA) led by Francis Ona and of the civil war.

Regan (2007) argues that the leadership of the New Panguna Landowners' Association 'were seeking neither permanent closure of the mine, nor the initiation of a secessionist struggle'. Rather Ona and others around him, such as PNG Defence Force (PNGDF) captain and explosives expert Sam Kauona, aspired to reopen the mine under a new income-sharing formula that might one day support an independent Bougainville. Some Panguna leaders we interviewed disagreed with this view, insisting that Ona really wanted to close the mine and rid Panguna of 'redskins', rather than simply increase the compensation. Regan (2007) himself concedes that some who joined Ona wanted to close the mine permanently. Probably greater numbers of supporters joined Ona's campaign around Panguna and Arawa because they wanted to end the social dislocation and sense of alienation caused by the huge presence of 'redskins' and Australians taking over their land. Finally, there were always secessionist advocates across Bougainville and they rushed in to seize the historical moment by supporting Ona. Many young men doubtless rallied to the rebellion for the excitement and status of evicting the foreigners and demolishing the symbols of their economic domination. People therefore joined the coalition that became the BRA for different reasons. And Ona was the kind of leader who promised them that they could all achieve their objectives.

Eugene Ogan argues that Ona could have used the crisis in a way we will see that Noah Musingku used it—as a strategy for averting arrest:

> [N]o one can know for sure whether [Ona's] motivations might have changed since his initial retreat to the bush, it is much more likely that his apparently political pronouncements represent tactics to extricate himself from a personal dilemma (he has been accused of murdering his patrilineal uncle, Matthew Kove [of the old Panguna Landowners' Association]) than a coherent plan to supplant any government authority. (Ogan 1990:37)[1]

If this was correct, the initiatives of the hawk faction of the PNG Government led by Ted Diro early in the crisis to put a large bounty on Ona's head, for example, might not have been the best strategies to keep the door open to early efforts to broker peace. Police riot squads were deployed to Bougainville in December 1988 from elsewhere in Papua New Guinea soon after the pylon explosions. Immediately there were allegations of brutality by these police, violence escalated and further riot squad police were flown in during January 1989. In March 1989, attacks on government and plantation buildings spread across Bougainville. In response, the first PNGDF troops were deployed to Bougainville later that month. A state-of-emergency on Bougainville was declared by the national government in June 1989. In July 1989, the first 'care centres' were established after villagers became homeless after police/PNGDF destruction of their homes. These were refugee camps where people who fled their homes were kept under surveillance. The care centres became part of the PNG counterinsurgency strategy. Six hundred villagers were evacuated from the mountains where they might provide food for the BRA and villages the BRA might merge into.

The original aims of Ona and his group were about the mine, about what landowners saw as the unjust share they received of the fruits of their land, but probably more fundamentally about the 'process of social disintegration' and environmental disintegration that the mine was causing (Filer 1992:116). It became something more—a call for secession—only after Ona's David versus Goliath performance struck a responsive chord across all of Bougainville and spontaneous attacks on government and foreign property erupted in many places in sympathy. This is not to say that support for the BRA was universal. In the north of the province in particular, and even in Arawa, there were educated elites who saw the economic advantages of integration with Papua New Guinea for the province and for their personal employment opportunities. The excesses of the security forces in response enhanced Ona's position as the bold leader who now would lead all Bougainville in a revolt to independence. There was

---

1 Anthony Regan does not think this is very likely, based on his more recent interviews. Moreover, he points out that while it is widely reported that Ona was responsible for the murder of Kove, many people in fact resented Kove for complex reasons. So, any analysis based on a fixed view of who killed Kove seems unwarranted. What is clear is that from very early in the conflict a condition of negotiation from the militant leadership was 'immunity from arrest' (Independent State of Papua New Guinea 1990:34).

nothing unusual about this policing excess. In the Highlands of New Guinea, it was standard practice for the riot police to burn villages in payback for violence. It became a routine tactic for both the police and the military in Bougainville to set fire to houses during patrols. Thousands of houses were razed. PNGDF officer Yauka Liria concluded this was counterproductive:

> If we can't get them, we'll get their homes was the general feeling ......
> The village, to a villager, is more than just shelter. It is his livelihood, his heritage, his pride. His village is at the centre of his heart. It has almost spiritual and religious significance in PNG society. You will never convince a Papua New Guinea villager who has sat on a hill and watched his village burn to ashes, that both you and he are on the same side. He will hate you for the rest of his life. (Yauka Liria, quoted in Dorney 1998:45)

Figure 3.1 Francis Ona (centre) holding the Japanese officer's sword captured in World War II that was part of his daily uniform, surrounded by BRA fighters

Photo: Ben Bohane

Cease-fire and early peace initiatives fail

From the outset, there were doves in PNG civil society and the national parliament who resisted the analysis of the hawks, who argued to Australian Foreign Minister, Gareth Evans, against the use of Australian helicopters and pilots in Bougainville. In 1989, the PNG Government appointed a Special Committee on the Crisis in the North Solomons Province, chaired by Sir John Kaputin, which investigated the conflict's origins and development and made various recommendations to the government on how to prevent escalation as its work progressed. The special committee consistently favoured a negotiated approach to resolving the crisis and was critical of the use of excessive force by the police and military. Kaputin was perhaps the first influential advocate of an international peacekeeping force (from the United Nations, the Commonwealth or the South Pacific Forum [now called the Pacific Islands Forum]) (Wolfers 2006b:11; Independent State of Papua New Guinea 1990:A-17, 74–5).

In February 1989, PNG Prime Minister, Rabbie Namaliu, attempted a cease-fire followed up by the offer in April of a new compensation package for Bougainville. Francis Ona was initially open and an agreement was reached, but PNG police undermined the accomplishment by arresting Ona's people as they left a celebration party and the cease-fire was spurned. When Prime Minister Namaliu announced the June 1989 state-of-emergency, he also announced a 'Peace Package' for Bougainville. The North Solomons Provincial Government under Premier, Joseph Kabui, had been preparing for this through a select committee chaired by Nasioi member John Bika designed to propose a high level of autonomy for Bougainville. Bika was murdered on 11 September 1989 by the BRA. Statements followed from Ona that Bika had undermined support for him and for secession. Bika was due to fly to Port Moresby the next day to sign with Prime Minister Namaliu the framework for a peace that included greatly increased revenue from the mine for Bougainville, including 5 per cent ownership of the mine by landowners and 5 per cent by the provincial government (Dorney 1998:45).

The Prime Minister convened a public peace ceremony attended by 1500 people, including the provincial premier, church and traditional leaders, in Arawa in October 1989. Nothing was accomplished, as Ona, who did not attend, rejected the peace package. In the same period, the Catholic Church was developing an initiative for peace talks and had been receiving positive responses from the PNG Government and the BRA. This effort also collapsed at this time. Escalation was the PNGDF response: 'Operation Footloose' from January 1990 was an all-out war on the BRA. This was intended to enable the national government to negotiate peace from a position of strength, but in fact the BRA got the upper hand over government forces. Graeme Kemelfield (1990) of the Buka campus of the University of Papua New Guinea put together a team of senior people in the provincial government at the beginning of 1990 who invited Swedish peace researcher Peter Wallensteen to attempt peace negotiations. Wallensteen and the team met with Sam Kaouna of the BRA. A cease-fire agreement was signed with remarkable ease between the BRA and the security forces in March 1990.

The PNGDF and police completely pulled out of Bougainville and Buka Islands in March 1990, though a presence was maintained on Nissan Island 60 km north of Buka (Havini 1992:162). Kemelfield (1990) and his team expected a gradual phase out of the PNGDF's presence. The international observer team to monitor the pullout flew in on the plane on which the last soldiers departed. They did stage a token surrender ceremony (Kemelfield 1990, 1992), though BRA military commander Kauona is reported to have said that '[w]e agreed to lay down our arms, but not to surrender them' (Oliver 1991:236). More than just withdraw the PNGDF, the national government pulled out all government services, resources and public servants. Banks and other businesses controlled from Papua New Guinea were closed and non-Bougainvilleans mostly left the province. An air and sea blockade on the supply of goods and services to Bougainville was imposed in May 1990. What gradually became apparent was that the most devastating aspect of the blockade for the lives of ordinary Bougainvilleans was that it included a blockade of medical supplies (Evans 1992; Gillespie 2009). Papua New Guinea suffered adverse international publicity over this, which ultimately became a factor in reconsideration of the blockade strategy. Meanwhile, Amnesty International in 1990 detailed the deaths of 19 people by extrajudicial execution or after being tortured in custody and 50 other cases of torture or ill treatment in Bougainville. These Amnesty numbers escalated greatly in subsequent reports as the war continued for seven more years.[2]

Government flight, ethnic flight: enter the Bougainville Interim Government

By mid 1990, a kind of ethnic cleansing had been achieved. With respect to 'redskins', this had been an important objective of many, but not all, among the coalition of interests who joined the BRA. There was a flight of nearly all of the many thousands of 'redskins' from the province and of white expatriates who worked for BCL. Hundreds from mainland Papua New Guinea who were married to Bougainvilleans stayed, however, including the wife of Francis Ona, and some

---

2   Between 1991 and November 1993, Amnesty International reported another 60 extrajudicial executions by the security forces, and between 1994 and January 1997, another 62, plus 13 disappearances of individuals taken into custody by the PNGDF. At the hands of the BRA, 36 deliberate killings were reported, though it was concluded that all these numbers were undoubtedly much higher (Amnesty International 1997).

others were adopted as Bougainvilleans. Some who stayed were victimised, but most were not, and some mainlanders fought in the BRA (Tanis 2002b). Today many whites and mainland New Guineans have returned, though not in the numbers of the 1970s and 1980s. A smaller group who never returned were the Chinese. There had been Chinatowns in Buka, Buin and Kieta. The Chinese were brought to Bougainville as indentured 'coolie' labour by German companies before World War I (Elder 2005:157). During our fieldwork in 2004, 2006 and 2007, we saw none, though John Braithwaite was told of one old Chinese man whom he had met in 1969 who was seeing out his days in a quiet place in the bush, there had been some Chinese intermarriage with Bougainvilleans and there were stories of Chinese collecting rent on stores in Buka. People in Buka spoke of one of the positives of the war as the flight of Chinese from running the shops of the old Chinatowns. It was clear the indigenous management of these shops was seen as a form of progress that Bougainville would not step back from.

The PNG Government's complete pullout and blockade in 1990 surprised the BRA. They thought they were winning the war on the ground against the PNGDF. They thought they had negotiated a cease-fire in which the PNGDF only would pull out, not the police and other services. In fact, the police pulled out first because the Police Commissioner was opposed to the cease-fire and feared his officers would be slaughtered without the protection of the army. This in turn provided the justification for punishing secessionism by completely withdrawing civil servants, who, with some justification, the government said could not be protected. Before departing, the police set all prisoners free, doubtless contributing to the *raskol* (semi-organised crime gangs) problem that took over the province. While there was steering by the Prime Minister and the Deputy Prime Minister of the strategy of allowing Bougainville to descend into chaos by punitive withdrawal of services and the blockade, it was in fact a strategy that unfolded from a process of independent decisions by what Filer (1992) called 'bits of the state'. By this Filer means subunits of the state, such as the police, fragments of the military or other pieces of the bureaucracy or elected officials, pursuing their own agenda rather than one set by cabinet. In this case, the most decisive bit of the state making its own decision was the police deciding to get out before the military left.

The BRA and its Bougainville Interim Government (BIG) nevertheless seized the moment and declared Bougainville independent as the Republic of Me'ekamui on 17 May 1990. Provincial Premier, Joseph Kabui, was appointed Vice-President of the BIG and Francis Ona President. But the Republic of Me'ekamui was not the inheritor of a state, or even bits of it, after the military pulled out. This was not at all like a coup in which those with the guns declare themselves the new government and take over the management of the old state structures.

Nothing much of the old state was left. The district office buildings that used to house the civil servants were left behind, but then the jubilant, undisciplined young men of the BRA burned them all! The BRA/BIG inherited considerable chaos and ungovernability. Indeed, young BRA fighters who were also surprised at their unexpected overnight victory created a large part of that chaos. Not everything in the mining town of Arawa was trashed at that point, though much of it was, and it was not long before every shop and building was burned out and looted—and many of the houses in the town as well. Vehicles were hijacked. Many women were harassed, especially those who it was believed were consorting with the security forces and those married to 'redskins'.

Decentralised governance through councils of chiefs was attempted at three tiers: clan, village and area councils of chiefs. But chiefs[3] were not always impressed that no resources were available for their work. The first priority of the BRA/BIG was basic security. They were organised as an insurgency, not as a government. Local commanders had autonomy to keep fighting their local war as an assurance against the BRA leadership being captured. Commanders in some localities had operated more as *raskol* gangs than as a liberation army. They stole from people. They could be arbitrary and capricious in the way they exacted revenge against those they believed might have collaborated with the PNGDF. Many innocent people were tortured and sexually assaulted. Some BRA commanders used their new monopoly of force on their patch to settle old disputes over land, sorcery, local economic inequalities and other grievances that had nothing to do with the BRA struggle. Relatively affluent villages in Buka and on the central eastern coast were sometimes targeted by BRA elements from poorer areas (Regan 2007). Theft of vehicles and other valuables was at times a motive for attacks on particular individuals or places. There was a trade to ship the items by barge to the Solomon Islands for sale (Regan 2007). There were even cases of scores being settled at various stages of the war that dated from World War II, when some communities supported the Japanese and others the Allies (Rimoldi and Rimoldi 1992:18). The chaos of decentralised insurgency and the absence of police allowed groups of armed young men to form for criminal or local political purposes and claim to be BRA. These 'skin BRA' terrorised many parts of Bougainville.

Chaos and the resistance

In time, divisions within the BRA at local levels began to open up cracks in the top leadership as confidence in Francis Ona's capacity to manage the situation he had fought for began to erode. As one Siwai woman put it in 1993: 'Francis

3   Chiefs are defined here as any form of traditional leader in Bougainville.

never came out openly and talked to the people. He just hid away in his little place up at Panguna.' Mid 1991 was a time when he particularly needed to be seen out among his people assuring them that order would be restored and that he had a plan for re-establishing security and good governance. Ona needed to be seen ordering the arrest of looters of government property. He needed to be public about punishing BRA fighters who raped women. His aloofness from his people also rendered him unaccountable to them in any informal, deliberative sense. He was a disengaged leader of dramatic gestures, not a man of practical action to solve his peoples' problems.

Many areas formed BRA groups to provide protection to their people from other BRA groups. In various other places, villagers began to arm to protect themselves locally against the predations of rogue BRA and/or skin BRA groups. Coalescence increased, particularly on Buka Island in the north, as such groups coordinated to form initially the Bougainville Resistance Group, later renamed the Bougainville Resistance Force (BRF). PNG intelligence welcomed this development and began to get support to the Resistance in money and weapons. From about 1992 onwards, the war shifted from one mostly between the BRA and the PNGDF to one mostly among Bougainvilleans—between the BRA and the Resistance (Boege 2006:6). In December 1990 – January 1991, fighting between the BRA and the Buka Liberation Front (BLF) raged all over Buka, with 'the PNGDF [who had returned to Buka by then] seemingly taking little part in proceedings' (Spriggs 1992:12). One reason why all this was opening up cracks in the BRA leadership was that many Resistance fighters were former BRA. Bougainville was shaking out into BRA areas, Resistance areas and neutral villages that sought to steer the difficult course of keeping out the BRA, the BRF and the PNGDF. Just as some BRA units had become *raskol* gangs, so too had some BRF units.

Between 1990 and 1992, former PNGDF commander Ted Diro, who for a period was Deputy Prime Minister, was the leader of a hawks' faction in the PNG Cabinet. This was also the period when the value of Australia's Defence Cooperation Program funding to support the war peaked. In 1990–91, it was at A$52 million—compared with its normal level of A$20 million a year (Claxton 1998:98). Australia supplied light and heavy weapons, aircraft, speedboats, mortars, bombs, helicopters and patrol boats and Australian military advisers were posted in Bougainville (Sharp 1997:2). Australia's mercenary laws were hastily relaxed to allow Australian and New Zealand civilian pilots to fly Iroquois helicopters provided to Papua New Guinea in 1989. The helicopters were used to drop BRA suspects into the sea, among other atrocities. Also in 1991, Australia belatedly began to come to the view that a military solution would not work. Diro and his hawks' analysis was that there were times when the BRA leadership was concentrated in Panguna and that it was possible to surround the mountain and totally decapitate the BRA political and military leadership. Private military contractor Sandline had a similar analysis in 1997. We have taken this analysis seriously in our research because it was advanced by sophisticated, highly trained military men of wide experience. It is certainly a conventional military view that insurgency leaders must meet at times if they are to coordinate well and, when they do, decapitation of the leadership can be effective. We put the Diro analysis to BRA leaders Kauona, Toroama and Kabui. It seems unlikely that if the PNG hawks had had their way in the early 1990s, even if backed by more Australian equipment and training, the BRA would have crumbled. Panguna was in fact only one of four BRA command centres. Leaders at the other three would almost certainly have continued the fight—indeed the imperative for them to do this had been discussed, should all the Panguna-area leaders be killed or captured. Joseph Kabui moved regularly from area to area.

The most dramatic local power struggle—the effects of which have still not healed today—occurred in the south-western district of Siwai. Siwai was a solidly pro-BRA district in the early stages of the war, but then a power struggle broke out in the early 1990s over local BRA leadership and strategy over the return of government services. Allegations of sorcery and disputes over unequal access to land were involved in the local split. One faction controlled the council of chiefs, the other a competing power structure. A group of chiefs on one side of the split invited the PNGDF in to protect them. They became BRF and fought with the PNGDF from the south against BRA control of the north of Siwai. While neither faction could initially martial the resources to deliver services to people, the faction that went with the Resistance became regionally formidable with financial support from Port Moresby. Nick Penniai, a leader of this group, became the first Speaker of the Bougainville Parliament in 2005 with support from his most prominent BRA enemy in Siwai, Jonathan Ngati, after a large reconciliation ceremony between the two that both claimed left them friends and healed. Power sharing did create incentives for reconciliations such as this that were not just skin deep. Most of the leaders who were at one another's throats in the Siwai crisis were, however, still not reconciled in 2008.

More failed peace processes

Attempts at peacemaking were almost continuous, even as fighting escalated. The first was Prime Minister Namaliu's Peace Package and large peace ceremony in October 1989 and the almost simultaneous initiative led by Father Leibert of the Catholic Church. In March 1990, the PNG Government, the BIG/BRA and officers of the PNG-backed Provincial Administration reached the cease-fire agreement in response to the more wide-ranging but unsuccessful peace agreement initiated by Graeme Kemelfield (1990, 1992). Further peace talks were held on the New Zealand Navy ship *Endeavour* in July and August 1990. Papua New Guinea interpreted the Endeavour Accord (Spriggs 1992:28–9), signed by Sir Michael Somare as head of the national government delegation and Joseph Kabui as head of the Bougainville delegation, as a plan for the restoration of government services with security provided for that restoration as needed by the PNGDF. The BRA interpreted it as agreement to the former without the PNGDF. But the PNGDF redeployed, though only into the island provincial capital of Buka across a narrow strait to the north of Bougainville Island in September 1990 in response to a plea from Buka leaders (in reality, it was only certain leaders) for a return of the PNGDF to protect them from the BRA. These leaders signed the Kavieng 'MOU [memorandum of understanding] Between Buka Community Leaders and the National Government Delegation' (Spriggs 1992:30–2). By mid 1991, the BLF forces supported by the PNGDF had effectively returned all Buka to PNG control.

Somare and Kabui and their delegations signed the 'Honiara Declaration' on 23 January 1991 (Spriggs 1992:33–41). It was an initiative sponsored by the Solomon Islands Government and the Solomon Islands Christian Association. This was a much more comprehensive agreement than had been signed in the 1990 Endeavour Accord. It committed to restoration of services, lifting the blockade and made councils of chiefs agents of an interim legal authority. The BRA agreed to surrender its arms under the supervision of a 'Multinational Supervisory Team'. The PNG Government agreed to amnesties for combatants. It did not contribute to ending the conflict, with the BRA refusing to surrender its weapons, as agreed in Honiara. BRA military commander Sam Kaouna argued that Joseph Kabui did not have the authority to make this agreement. Neither side honoured much of its part of the agreement. BRA torture and murder of Bougainvilleans who had once worked for the civil service—many of them in fact BRA supporters—that had begun in 1990 were now causing a problem for the BRA/BIG, especially for those who wanted a return of government services, which the people were pleading for. But the BRA was divided on this issue; many did not want a return of government services in any guise. This divide was an important factor in the Siwai crisis. The civil service in Bougainville became in this context an influential 'bit of the state' (Filer 1992) because it was unwilling to go along with a peace agreement that put it in the firing line.

On 13 April 1991, the PNGDF launched its second invasion of Bougainville Island across from Buka in breach of the Honiara Declaration, without the approval or support of Cabinet. From this point on, the military was decreasingly under political control from Port Moresby. Local commanders were often fighting their own private little wars 'that followed the logic of pay back more than instructions from the government in far away Port Moresby' (Boege 2006:7). The reoccupation gradually moved south, with occasional skirmishes based on the same strategy that had restored PNG control to Buka. Resistance forces formed locally—in many instances, from former BRA members. They asked the PNGDF to support them in the removal of the BRA and criminal gangs from their lands. The Resistance was armed and supported with other resources from the government. The PNGDF and Resistance pushed the BRA to retreat from control of areas where local chiefs invited the PNGDF in, which the BRA mostly did without a fight. A reconciliation meeting was then held between the local community and the PNGDF. In many cases, the PNGDF just secured enclaves of control surrounded by areas of BRA control. A second front with this strategy was also opened up by a sea landing at Siwai in the south-west, exploiting the divisions that had split open the BRA in Siwai. A PNGDF colonel told us that many of the pacified spaces they created as they moved south fell apart behind them because the PNG Government failed to follow-up by restoring government services after the local peace was established. As the army moved south, the BRA often melted away in front of them, then flowed back around them to the north to reoccupy pacified areas.

Hardline Prime Minister Wingti and the succession of an impatient peacemaker

This strategy did not work in the Nasioi districts of central Bougainville where Francis Ona had started the war. But when hardliner Paias Wingti took over as PNG Prime Minister and increased funding for the Bougainville campaign, PNGDF hawks opted for a new strategy of advancing into the Nasioi heartland of the BRA without invitation from local communities. Arawa was reoccupied in February 1993 after some weeks of moving up from the Loloho area; in August 1994, Wingti prematurely announced the recapture of the mine area around Panguna. But the PNGDF held the area only briefly. The PNGDF suffered many reversals and losses from the insurgency in mountainous jungle where visibility for patrols was only a few metres. Amnesty International also reported a dramatic increase in extrajudicial executions by the military in 1993 (Amnesty International 1997).

Wingti was not in favour of peace talks and rejected the promise in earlier agreements that the BRA would be offered an amnesty. Yet behind the scenes another bit of state, the Department of Foreign Affairs, led by its new minister, Sir Julius Chan, was winning support among South Pacific nations to establish a South Pacific Peacekeeping Force. While the South Pacific Forum rejected the proposal at that time, the seed of what ultimately became a South Pacific peacekeeping operation on Bougainville was planted by this diplomacy. The head of the Department of Foreign Affairs had discussions with representatives of the BRA/BIG in Honiara chaired by Solomons Island Prime Minister, Francis Billy Hilly, in mid 1994.

We will see in the next chapter that Sir Julius Chan became a catalyst of important peace initiatives. But when he became impatient with their frustrating progress, he triggered a near catastrophe by contracting mercenaries to break the deadlock.

4. Peacemaking on, off and finally back on track

Arawa Peace Conference, 1994

Sir Julius Chan became PNG Prime Minister in September 1994. Worried that the defence forces might sabotage his peace initiatives, Chan immediately took ministerial control of both the military and the police. Within days of taking over, Chan was in Honiara, Solomon Islands, for talks with BRA military commander Sam Kauona chaired by Solomons Prime Minister Billy Hilly. They signed the Honiara Commitments on a cease-fire and peace conference in Arawa with security provided for people from all over Bougainville to attend by a South Pacific Peacekeeping Force. Australia funded this mostly non-Australian force named Operation Lagoon with leadership provided by Australian Brigadier Peter Abigail and colonels from Tonga, Fiji and Vanuatu.

But after Kauona reported back to Francis Ona, the BRA began to backtrack. Ona objected to the force being led by an Australian. Brigadier Abigail and the three Pacific colonels visited Ona in the mountains to give him their personal assurance that they could guarantee his security. But Ona had never attended any of the peace conferences and was not going to start at Arawa. His most senior deputies, Kauona and Kabui, also did not attend. Senior commander Ishmael Toroama did attend, but was attacked by the PNGDF in the process; one of his aides was wounded (Breen 2001a:73–5). It is doubtful whether Ona or the rest of the leadership group ever intended to show. Without Ona, and with Kauona now deeply distrusted by Chan and most of the national and international players because he walked away from his signature on the Honiara Commitments, nothing concrete was achieved at Arawa in 1994. Australian Prime Minister, Paul Keating, and other regional leaders cancelled their plans to attend the finale. From a military point view, Operation Lagoon in 1994 was not a model peace operation (Breen 2001a). Beyond Sir Julius Chan's rushed political timetable for it, the fundamental problem was military: elements of the PNGDF were not under the authority of their prime minister and cabinet; they were a 'bit of the state' executing plans to attack and kill BRA attending the conference. Even an Australian helicopter was fired on and hit—almost certainly by PNGDF troops.

Yet the Arawa Peace Conference succeeded in accelerating momentum towards peace by allowing 1200 members of civil society from across Bougainville to assemble and commit to peace (Breen 2001a). Talk to officers of the South Pacific Peacekeeping Force and they say they went home feeling they failed utterly; talk to civil society leaders, particularly women's leaders, and many see the Arawa Peace Conference as a turning point to peace. It allowed the women to coordinate the talking in of local fighters across all Bougainville and the winding of women's peace marches across the island. It was the moment when the Bougainvillean Women's Choir sang *Island of Sorrow*, written by one of their members, Elizabeth Burein. The sound of this lament brought tears many times to those who cared about peace in Bougainville. It came to symbolise a turning point to hope:

> *Bougainville is an island, an island of sorrow.*
> *Bougainville is an island, an island of pain.*
> *There are people dying, there are people crying.*
> *Who is responsible?*
> *There's no education, there's no hospital.*
> *Who is responsible?*
> *There are people dying, there are people crying.*
> *Not knowing why. Bougainville island is an island I love.*

It was sung opposite the burnt-out buildings of Bougainville's largest hospital under a tree in the grounds of the gutted Arawa High School, which had not seen students in years. The women were more determined, patient, persistent and resilient than Sir Julius Chan. Chan had wanted Arawa to be his triumph and he wanted a result in Bougainville before he faced the people in an election to consolidate his ascendency after the vote of no confidence in Wingti.

The North Nasioi peace zone

A second bottom-up success of Arawa was that it created a new 'island of civility' (Kaldor 1999) within the surrounding heartland region of the war. North Nasioi traditional leaders and BRA commanders attended Arawa and then established a North Nasioi peace zone from which they hoped peace would spread. These leaders followed up on Arawa locally by signing a peace agreement with the national government. Our interviews suggested that their hopes were realised that they would demonstrate to neighbouring districts that their peace could deliver safe streets, get more food in people's mouths, get trade moving, get children back in school and health care delivered. Theodore Miriung was a former acting National Court judge and local intellectual who articulated this vision of peace rippling out from their local peace zone. He did so with an intolerance of those with less vision; this was softened, however, by the leadership he shared with outstanding women such as Josephine Harepa.[1] Ultimately, multiple islands of civility did spread and merge until the islands of incivility became exceptions that the Truce and Peace Monitoring Groups could later join to the peace in the following way:

> If there was a particularly violent or troublesome village that we weren't able to go to, we would go to all the villages around it and then basically send out the message that we were not going to go to your village if you were going to be like that. We'd use the women's network to send out that message and the women would then shame the men into behaving and then we would visit. (Interview with Australian peacekeeper, 2008)

The North Nasioi island of civility was, therefore, just one of many islands of civility. Yet it had the special significance of throwing up, in the words of Anthony Regan, 'a leadership option that bridged the BRA–BRF gap'. The North Nasioi Peace Committee worked at reconciliation and communication among the divided leadership of Central Bougainville. In the days after the Arawa conference, Miriung twice made the risky journey to Ona in the mountains to plead unsuccessfully with him to come back with him to Arawa to join the peace process. In Port Moresby, Health Minister, Sir Peter Barter, was the leader with the vision to see the crucible of hope in the work of the North Nasioi Peace Committee. He became a family friend of the Miriungs and collaborator with Miriung's peace vision. Anthony Regan, an academic from The Australian National University whose sister had married a Bougainvillean, also became a collaborator with the Miriung–Barter peace path until Miriung's death and beyond it in the form of the Barter Peace Plan.

---

1   During our fieldwork, Josephine Harepa was manager of the Arawa Women's Training Centre. The centre runs the best visitor's accommodation in Arawa and many peace meetings and visiting peacebuilders stayed there. Before establishing the centre with UNDP funding, the more conservative North Nasioi women who were early movers to peace with Miriung at the end of the 1990s had joined hands with the more radical, pro-BRA Women for Peace and Freedom, who in the mid 1990s also became active in persuading BRA fighters to join the peace. So the joining together of the North Nasioi peacemakers with the peacemakers of the Bougainville Women for Peace and Freedom subsequently expanded the zone of peace out from this node where peacemakers could gather.

Figure 4.1 Women organised peace marches all over Bougainville. This is in fact a photo of women organising children playing bamboo flutes in a march to welcome peacekeepers to a reconciliation ceremony in the grounds of King Tore's 666 Movement in Nagovis in 2000

Photo: Ben Bohane

Miriung's Bougainville Transitional Government

November 1994 saw Miriung and Chan sign the Mirigini Charter, which pledged leaders of the national government and the people of Bougainville to continue the peace process started at Arawa. The idea was to establish a Bougainville Transitional Government based on an assembly of leaders 'nominated by councils of chiefs'. In April 1995, a Bougainville Transitional Government was established as a successor to the North Solomons Provincial Government, which had been suspended in 1990. Seats covered all of Bougainville, with three intentionally left vacant for areas fully under BRA control. The idea was that they would eventually be occupied by Ona, Kabui and Kauona (Dorney 1998:55). The assembly voted Theodore Miriung Premier. Miriung believed that with patience he could eventually entice the BRA leadership to join the transitional government in negotiating a political settlement. Miriung's problem was that Chan (and the PNGDF) and Ona (and his hardline supporters) both saw him as untrustworthy and coopted by the other side.

Miriung secured Chan's agreement to grant amnesty for actors on both sides who committed crimes during the conflict, to negotiate for autonomy for Bougainville and to convene meetings to build consensus for peace on the BRA side of the conflict. September 1995 saw the Transitional Government meet with BRA/BIG representatives in Cairns, together with representatives of the Solomon Islands and Australia. Ona did not attend. At another December meeting in Cairns, Kauona and Kabui (again without Ona) met with Miriung and the Bougainville Transitional Government, representatives of the United Nations and the Commonwealth Secretariat to discuss steps to peace and humanitarian assistance. On returning to Bougainville in January 1996, the BRA/BIG representatives came under fire from PNG security forces. Spoilers (Stedman 1997) were on the loose. The BRA's Ishmael Toroama led savage retaliatory attacks to end the cease-fire. This was some of the most deadly fighting of the war. The BRA gained the upper hand. Disastrous setback though this was, the Cairns meetings helped build relationships among the key players from Bougainville that laid a foundation for the truce that would ultimately come at Burnham two years later. They also built experience in coming to grips with the positions of others and reality testing of some of their own unrealistic positions. Brisbane lawyers Mark Plunkett and Leo White helped to build on the legacy in 1997 with conflict-resolution training for BRA and BIG members. This reinforced Miriung's work in bridging the gaps between the key Bougainville players that were often based on misconceptions of one another's positions.

In 1996, Miriung developed a modified version of the councils of chiefs, called councils of elders, which would foster 'a symbiotic relationship between customary authority and state authority' (Regan 2002a). They would ground the state in the legitimacy of customary authority and underwrite customary authority with the legitimacy of the state. Citizens of a council of elders' area would opt every five years to select their elders by election or by custom (which could include heredity). This would allow areas to undergo smooth transitions to more democratic from more traditional hierarchical forms of authority. The term 'elders' rather than 'chiefs' was opted for so that church leaders, women's leaders, youth leaders and others could also join chiefs in leadership roles. All 40 councils had at least one female member in 2007. The growth of women's voices was seen as an objective of the reform. Bougainville has a recent history of competition between traditional chiefs and more modern forms of leadership based on education and entrepreneurship (Regan 2000:300). Miriung's reforms were based on power sharing that would strengthen traditional and more education-oriented and market-oriented forms of leadership. Paul Johnson's account of English legal reforms in the early Middle Ages is brought to mind: 'The present is reformed by rewriting the past in such a way that it becomes the future' (quoted by John Connell in Regan 2000:302).

The councils would facilitate bottom-up planning, do much local administration and empower most of the dispute resolution and legal decision making at the local level. Chiefs would be especially responsible for reconciliation and reintegration of combatants. Miriung enlisted the Peace Foundation Melanesia to do leadership training with chiefs in exerting 'power with' as opposed to what he saw as older patterns of 'power over' (Howley 2002:86–7). The law for the councils of elders that passed the provincial legislature in 1996 also provided for village assemblies of all customary landowning groups in the village area (Regan 2000). In many, but not all, areas these are functioning well today and are potentially the most vibrant level of governance (Boege 2008:28). Councils of elders still cover most parts of Bougainville today, though their success has been uneven and nowhere have they been adequately resourced. During the conflict there were no resources. Post-conflict, leaders of the Autonomous Bougainville Government naturally favoured channelling scarce resources to building their new state administrative structures—and this fitted the state-building ethos of donors.

Theodore Miriung is still seen by many in Bougainville as a visionary whose inspiration survives and struggles into the future. He was assassinated in front of his family in October 1996. Largely suppressed investigations into the premier's assassination make it fairly clear that elements of the PNGDF working with the Siwai Resistance planned the murder. While Miriung's assassination extinguished a flame of hope, it did push other moderates to step up and it created a vacancy for a new visionary leader of Bougainville who could only be a high-level member of Francis Ona's circle. That man eventually was Joseph Kabui. The transformative civil-society push for peace triggered by the 1994 Arawa Peace Conference—in the face of another top-down failure by Ona to participate in an important peace process—began to sow seeds of doubt in the mind of the other inner-circle leaders: Kauona, Kabui, Toroama and Ona's young secretary, James Tanis (who in December 2008 would succeed Kabui as President of the Autonomous Bougainville Government). Perhaps, they began to think, Ona would never deliver Bougainville the peace the people were demanding.

Sandline

Military spoilers were at work in the unsuccessful attempt to murder the BRA leaders returning from the Cairns peace talks and the successful attempt to murder Miriung. They were also embarked on a paradoxical process of winning the Prime Minister over to their military solution, but not in a way that proved to their liking. Between these two murderous episodes, in March 1996, the PNG Government made its first contact with Sandline International, a British military contracting organisation that in turn employed the South African private military organisation Executive Outcomes.[2] This led to a contract for the pacification of Bougainville (Dinnen et al. 1997; Dorney 1998; O'Callaghan 1999).

Military leaders on the ground in Bougainville were unaware of this and in July 1996 pushed ahead with another attempted surge: Operation High-Speed II. It ended in stalemate in August with many casualties on both sides. September 1996 saw the biggest loss of life of the PNGDF in a single operation of the war, with 12 members of the security forces killed in the Kangu Beach massacre (Box 4.1). As the details of this story gradually reached the press—especially that payback for rape of Bougainvillean women by soldiers addled with home-brew was involved—it further sapped morale in Port Moresby and confidence in the discipline and competence of their military. The electorate was deeply concerned that the war was lurching from one disaster to another and would go on forever. The Prime Minister and his inner circle had totally lost confidence in the PNGDF.

Box 4.1 The Kangu Beach massacre

Kangu Beach in the far south was one of the worst care centres. Bougainvilleans suffered much abuse there, including sexual assault of women. Chosen women were asked to carry food and water up to soldiers in a bunker above the care centre in the evening. After occupying them there for a while, soldiers would tell the women they would be in breach of curfew if they returned down the mountain. Soldiers then raped the women during the night.

We were able to interview some key PNG security force players and all of the local BRA hierarchy (except the murdered Paul Bobby), who were looking on at this situation with concern. They developed several plans to entice the Resistance to defect back to the BRA. The most successful element of these plans was placing an undercover BRA operative who had relatives at Kangu Beach into the Resistance there in 1994. This man was an effective leader and was promoted by the PNGDF to command of the Resistance at Kangu Beach. He remained surrounded by men loyal to the PNGDF. Various strategies to steer their loyalties back to the BRA failed. The women were the primary victims of abuse and were initially much more receptive to BRA appeals to defect back. Some widows and wives of Resistance men put their bodies on the line for the sake of other women by agreeing to have sex with soldiers. They then told their male relatives they had been raped. Combined with the earlier sexual violence, this finally turned the male Resistance leadership against the PNGDF.

---

2   The relationship between Sandline, Executive Outcomes and the multinational mining interests that were backing them remains murky. It appears that in some ways Sandline could have been a successor proxy to Executive Outcomes when the mining interests that backed Executive Outcomes perceived its reputation in Africa to be tarnished.

Then women of Kangu Beach, including some very young women, laid their bodies on the line in a second way on 8 September 1996. They got soldiers drunk. They then enticed the soldiers to put their weapons down to move down the beach to play volleyball with them. The defecting Resistance men were waiting to grab their weapons. On a signal, the women hit the sand and the PNG soldiers were mown down. Other women distracted soldiers elsewhere, keeping them away from their weapons. The commander was shot in his bed, others in the bunker. Twelve soldiers and PNG police were killed; five others surrendered—spared as hostages. A number of the bodies were found mutilated, 'several having their penises severed and shoved in their mouths' (Dorney 1998:140).

While the story of Bougainville women as leaders in the peace process is much told, the story of their physical bravery in putting their bodies on the line, as at Kangu Beach, is less told (Charlesworth 2008:352–4). The peacemaking story is partly about women going out into the bush to persuade male fighters to join the peace in circumstances where men were afraid that if they did they would be shot as spies by one side or the other. Some women peacemakers were killed—such as Angelina Nuguitu, of the Peace Foundation Melanesia, who was killed near Kangu Beach while trying to broker peace a month before the massacre. The five hostages became a major negotiating chip for the BRA. Even more importantly, the armoury they captured at Kangu Beach contained more than 60 automatic weapons, a great deal of ammunition, grenades, an 80 mm mortar, and more. While these weapons were boxed during the peace process, the BRA commander who captured them, Thomas Tari, has not destroyed the weapons and on occasion has broken the boxes open. His control of these weapons has made Tari a dominant warlord of sorts in the south. Tari's right-hand man executed his BRA superior in the south, Paul Bobby, and Bobby's brother in 1998.

Kangu Beach was a turning point of the war in various respects. It triggered an Australian Defence Department review of whether Australia had erred in allowing the PNGDF since 1991 to struggle through the war without determined Australian defence assistance. The review concluded Australia should continue to sit on the sidelines. The loss of life, the new bargaining chip of the five hostages and the captured weapons all shifted the momentum of the war in favour of the BRA. Morale in Port Moresby collapsed. The Prime Minister lost confidence in his army, and in Australia, and turned to Sandline. The PNGDF blamed Theodore Miriung, totally erroneously, for orchestrating the Kangu Beach massacre, because, coincidentally, he had visited the care centre that week. Many believe this is the reason they assassinated him.

Sandline International spent much of 1996 in communication with the PNG Defence Minister, Mathias Ijape, about mercenary assistance for the PNGDF to dislodge the BRA. Options were considered to mount the invasion jointly with the PNGDF supporting Sandline and with Rio-Tinto dollars and/or an income stream from a future joint venture to reopen the mine between the government, Sandline and Rio-Tinto's operating company (BCL) or some new operator. Lieutenant-Colonel (retired) Tim Spicer of Sandline prepared a consultancy report on options during 10 days in Papua New Guinea in which he pitched a grandiose vision of cargo arriving to fill the coffers of a strongman state:

> PNG is potentially one of the world's richest countries per capita…If its mineral wealth…is fully realised it could give the country the economic power to threaten Australia and dwarf all other economies in the region. If this wealth was combined with a well-trained, effective and combat-experienced military, then the country could become a very significant regional power. (*Spicer Report*, quoted in Dorney 1998:164)

Spicer argued that there had been a conspiracy by the other regional powers to keep Papua New Guinea weak: 'It is possible that there is a deliberate policy on the part of Australia and New Zealand to prolong the Bougainville problem, either by omission or commission.' The lack of direct military assistance from them was taken as evidence, along with Australian and New Zealand support only for resolution through 'negotiations/peaceful means'. Perhaps Australia played into this stereotype because, as one senior Australian intelligence official put it, when it became aware of Sandline, 'Australia had to do some heavying'. This included intervening to prevent weapons arriving for the mercenaries— to intercept them if necessary—because it 'could have been explosive to have these weapons arrayed against the PNGDF'.

Prime Minister Chan eventually was won over to a joint Sandline/PNGDF operation to capture Panguna and kill or capture the BRA leadership. A contract with Sandline was signed 31 January 1997. In February 1997, BCL shares dramatically jumped on the Australian stock exchange, which probably meant insider trading from the very small number of people who knew about the plan at that stage (Claxton 1998:69–70). There were also allegations of corrupt payments by both pro-Sandline and anti-Sandline interests that were in no case proved (Claxton 1998:70). Three weeks later, the story was broken by Mary-Louise O'Callaghan in *The Australian*, and PNG opposition followed in the wake of international opposition to such a costly and bloody military resolution. On 2 March, Chan announced his intention to purchase control of BCL as part of the Sandline-funding strategy.

PNGDF commander Jerry Singirok initially supported the plan, but then switched to the view that spending such vast resources on foreign mercenaries would be less effective in the long run than investing those resources in the PNGDF. Singirok simply wrote to the Prime Minister advising him that he had cancelled the joint operation with Sandline, surprised the Sandline personnel, put them under arrest and called a press conference before the prime minister had received the letter to announce his defiance of a prime minister who was planning to 'mortgage the island of Bougainville and other resource-rich areas to foreigners'. There was no call for Chan to resign nor for a commission of inquiry into the Sandline fiasco at first, though these demands came later amid large street demonstrations. This was a case of the crowd making history (Rudé 1964). It was a particular kind of crowd massing outside the Parliament in 1997 that was made up substantially of members of the military. There were also many non-governmental organisation (NGO) activists, students and ordinary people who were concerned about a mercenary onslaught on the people of Bougainville. In most cases where people power changes history, the crowd can effect regime change only when it coopts a military that declines to crush it. The Sandline street demonstrations reversed this people-power dynamic, with the military in effect coopting the demonstrations. A commission of inquiry was established and Chan did step aside for a period and then contested an election on the issue. Chan took to the airwaves to accuse Singirok of 'gross insubordination, bordering on treason' and of the possibility that he was 'attempting a coup' (Dorney 1998:292). A stand-off between the prime minister and defence commander threw the nation into a major crisis.

Australia backed the authority of the elected Prime Minister to sack his defence commander, but implicitly threatened withdrawal of aid if Papua New Guinea did not terminate the Sandline contract and deport its fighters. Eventually they were deported. Australian aircraft had intercepted the heavy equipment flown in for Sandline, forcing the Russian-built freighter down in Darwin. Prime Minister, John Howard, and his military advisors did not think Sandline would succeed militarily and feared the destabilising impact of mercenary intervention in the region.

In the 1997 PNG election, six of the nine cabinet ministers who attended the National Security Council Meeting that approved the hiring of Sandline lost their seats, including Chan.

Hardliners for a renewed PNGDF push for victory were still at work in July 1997 when New Zealand intelligence helped prevent a PNG ambush of BRA/ BIG leaders returning from the peace talks in New Zealand, though the PNGDF was suspected of responsibility for the murder of one moderate delegate with BRA links soon after his return from New Zealand (Regan 2005a). Most PNGDF, however, were war weary by then; many PNGDF officers were part of the moderate majority pressing for peace after the push of Operation High Speed II had failed and the Sandline intervention had collapsed. Sandline paved the path to a peace process that delivered.

In October 1998, international arbitrators found the Sandline contract valid and awarded Sandline US$25 million in payments, though Mary-Louise O'Callaghan (1999:366) estimates a total payment was made to Sandline of US$43 million without them ever having to fire a shot to earn it.

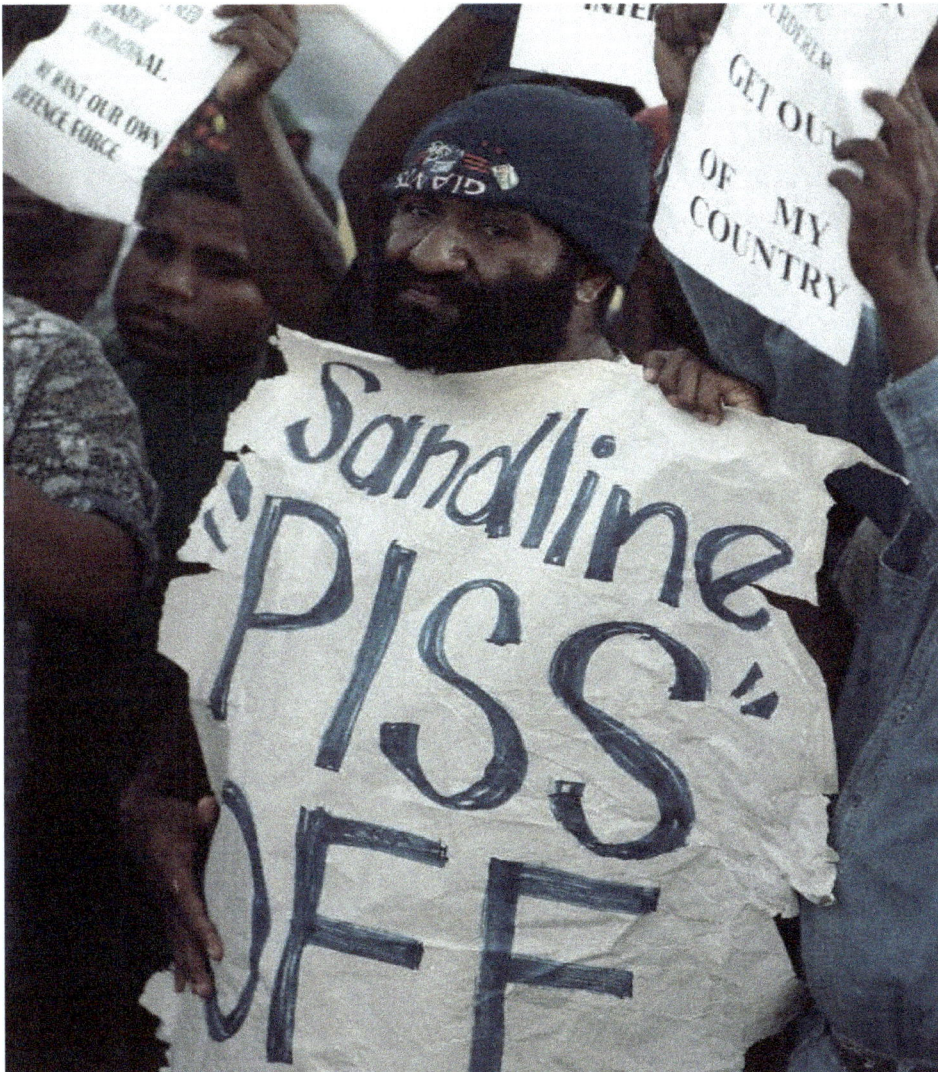

Figure 4.2 Port Moresby protestors against Sandline, 1997—a global turning point back to the anti-mercenary norm

Photo: AAP/AFP

New Zealand peace diplomacy

The interregnum between the stepping aside of Chan and the election of a new prime minister was one of productive peace diplomacy. On 28 May 1997, the National Executive Council approved Sir Peter Barter's Bougainville Peace Strategy. Barter had been unsuccessfully attempting to broker peace[3] since Miriung's assassination and the PNGDF attacks on Kauona and Kabui returning from Cairns.

Almost all parties to the conflict beyond the desperate politicians who signed the Sandline contract were united in their opposition to solving the conflict with mercenaries. This created a moment of unanimity among the PNGDF, BRA, Resistance and Bougainville political leaders of all stripes (Reddy 2006:228). Most critically, it changed BRA perceptions of who their enemies were and allowed moderates in the BRA and moderates in the PNG Parliament to find common cause (Regan 2010). The Sandline mutiny created a political space for an aggressive diplomatic initiative led by New Zealand Foreign Minister, Don McKinnon. He sent former New Zealand High Commissioner to Papua New Guinea John Hayes to lobby during the PNG election campaign for what became the breakthrough Burnham talks of July 1997. Burnham was a military base on the South Island of New Zealand. Burnham I was among just the Bougainville factions. It is important to see it not as something New Zealand initiated but as something the Bougainville leaders were planning (to resume the process they started in Townsville) and that New Zealand facilitated. Almost 100 Bougainville leaders, including women's leaders, attended. Kauona and Kabui were once more willing to participate, as was the new Premier of the Bougainville Transitional Government, Gerard Sinato, and the MPs from Bougainville just elected to the new PNG Parliament. These included senior minister John Momis, who had been captured by Ona loyalists during the 1997 election campaign. It was a near-run thing that he was not killed, with James Tanis eventually persuading Ona to release Momis. Ona, however, was still not willing to attend peace talks and Hayes' helicopter was fired on when it flew past Ona's Guava village on its way to pick up other BRA leaders for discussions.

Finally the time had come for a majority of the leaders of the BRA to separate from Ona. Ona's aloofness from the practical politics of the people and the rebellion resulted in a gradual process of Kauona becoming a more dominant leader during much of the war and in turn a gradual process of Kabui becoming the major figure in the diplomacy for peace. Ishmael Toroama, the BRA commander most respected by the troops on the ground, was also a quietly effective figure in supporting the peace against Ona's resistance. This now-moderate core of

---

3   Though Chan had been pretending to support Barter's peace diplomacy as a cover as he prepared the way for Sandline.

the BRA—like the moderate core of the Resistance—was worried about the corrosive effect of the conflict on the unity of Bougainville and the shared identity as Bougainvilleans that had blossomed before the Resistance coalesced (Regan 2010). An important lesson for BRA moderates resulted from an order from the BRA leadership not to accept Red Cross 'village packs' and 'family packs' of seeds, agricultural tools, blankets, cooking pots, and so on. In late 1996 and early 1997, villages in BRA-controlled areas defied the leadership to accept these packs (Regan 2010). BRA moderates feared that the next step for such communities could be for them to defect to the Resistance or become covert supporters of reintegration with Papua New Guinea.

Burnham differed from previous talks in including quite a wide circle of leaders, who came to understand and commit to the peace process. The Burnham I talks accomplished the first step towards the release of the five PNG security personnel still held hostage after the Kangu Beach massacre. Against considerable opposition, Kabui, with support from Toroama, coaxed agreement from the Bougainville factions to hand them over. Then there was a second difficult negotiation on the ground with Thomas Tari—who had custody of the five and was not at Burnham—led by Kabui and Hayes. For the new Prime Minister, Bill Skate, being able to welcome the five back to Port Moresby was a great confidence-building measure for the peace. Sam Akoitai had emerged from the war as the political leader of the Resistance and had been elected in the 1997 poll for the National Parliament. He was effective in putting pressure on Skate for support for the Burnham peace process in return for Akoitai's support in assuming the prime ministership. Akoitai became Skate's Minister for Bougainville Affairs and a major force in the peace process and in reconciliation between the BRA and the Resistance.

The Burnham I talks involved key national players such as Akoitai and Momis, but not the PNGDF. The talks were fundamentally about achieving the beginnings of a solid reconciliation for peace within Bougainville. They lasted 10 days and involved a traditional *tarout* or vomiting session in which 'unrestrained emotional outpourings are allowed to happen...[and] anything that any relevant party feels needs to be said, shouted or cried out is expressed' (Reddy 2006:227)—a kind of venting of psychological poisons. One of Peter Reddy's 2004 interviews captured the spirit of the early part of Burnham I:

> There were no specific procedures—we went into the room with NZDF in between our factions—we were ready to throw punches. The vomiting session united us and from then on we stood back as one. The BRA and the BIG were housed together, but separate from the Resistance. There was real enmity. It was really very difficult. Someone would shout to another person, 'You shot my brother, you murdered my brother'. And they would jump across to do violence but the NZ military were in

between. This went on until nothing was left inside. The women played a very important role, they would say 'Look, I am here, there is my son over there, and over there is my other son. And all of you, you are all our sons.' During this time there was no agenda and it was so important to vomit it all out. (Reddy 2006:228)

During that first five days of *tarout*, the women from the two sides were the ones who were crossing the divide between the BRA and Resistance living areas and forming joint agendas for peace that transcended the BRA–Resistance divide. A second round of peace talks at the Burnham military barracks in October 1997, with PNG leaders this time, eventually produced a truce. Since the movement to peace was flowing around the intransigence of the BRA leader, Francis Ona, both Burnham talks wisely involved the participation of dozens of young BRA and Resistance commanders from all corners of Bougainville. The Bougainville delegation at Burnham II numbered 80. New Zealand and Australian diplomats worried that this would be unwieldy and costly—a worry that proved misplaced. It was important that the younger commanders who attended the talks did not become spoilers of the peace. The movement from Burnham I to Burnham II was from trust building among the Bougainville factions to a truce between PNG and more unified Bougainville parties.

The next major meeting was even more widely participatory than the Burnham meetings. It was held at Lincoln University, New Zealand, in January 1998. During Burnham I and II and the Lincoln talks, a strong consensus emerged on the importance of an international peace force to nurture the peace process.

Conclusion: the diplomacy of flipping disasters into opportunities

A former Australian High Commissioner to Papua New Guinea described the sequence of New Zealand meetings as 'a brilliant piece of diplomacy by New Zealand'. He was aggravated by the way it played to the stereotype of 'Australia as clumsy, cultural insensitives of the Pacific', but conceded in the circumstances this stereotyping and the launching of the initiative as totally New Zealand's 'was actually helpful' in getting a result. 'In general,' he said, 'effective diplomacy involves avoiding coming in on a white charger. It's more like being a shepherd. Trying to herd all the key players to move in a positive direction, to keep them in the same paddock. It's frustrating, facilitating work' and New Zealand did it well. The former Australian High Commissioner also said when Miriung was assassinated, 'good diplomacy was about calming', keeping the Barter agenda alive in the capital and 'trying to move Momis and Akoitai to take constructive initiatives, which they did'. But in particular, good diplomacy is 'about taking advantage of disasters. That was why New Zealand diplomacy after Sandline was so brilliant.' One commentator said of this part of our text that 'New Zealand was building on what Miriung initiated and what Barter, Kabui, Akoitai and others were able to carry through'. Indeed, the lens of the diplomat in Port Moresby is just one lens and the one that focuses on the conversations that occurred among these players on Bougainville could be the more important one.

Sandline was an important historical event not only because the reaction against it brought the Burnham peace together. Until the mid 1990s, there had been an anti-mercenary norm in international affairs that had been particularly strong since the American Revolution—in fact, so strong that even in circumstances in which generals were desperate, they mostly refrained from hiring mercenaries when it would have been rational for them to do so (Percy 2007). The end of the Cold War and the neo-liberal spirit of the 1990s created a new environment of opportunity for mercenaries. Sandline and Executive Outcomes were the most important companies in the military business. They led what were seen as successful private military operations funded by seizing natural-resource assets in Angola and Sierra Leone in the mid 1990s (Percy 2007:209–11). Bougainville turned this tide decisively, as it was such an unmitigated failure for Sandline, the PNG Government and their corporate mining associates in the background with an interest in taking over the Bougainville mine. Bougainville helped to sharply reinstate the international anti-mercenary norm as the handiwork of Executive Outcomes and Sandline in Africa began to be reinterpreted negatively through the prism of the 'blood diamonds' corporate social responsibility debate. As their (allegedly shared [Percy 2007:213–14]) corporate backers from the mining sector distanced themselves, Executive Outcomes closed its doors in 1999, Sandline in 2004. But the principals of these companies such as Tim Spicer were back with a new business model in Iraq and Afghanistan. The private military corporation was dead, especially after the imprisonment of mercenary Simon Mann and the attempted extradition of Mark Thatcher in Africa. But the private security corporation that supported the militaries of major powers (instead of dominating the militaries and states of minor nations) boomed. While Bougainville was decisively important in resuscitating an international anti-mercenary norm that was eroding until 1997, the other reason why the anti-mercenary norm was reinstated was that a more profitable opportunity arrived with the war on terror for the entrepreneurs who who had been dismantling the anti-mercenary norm.

5. The architecture of the peace

The Truce and Peace Monitoring Groups

For a number of years, the BRA had been working towards internationalising the conflict through various UN agencies. So when an international monitoring force was agreed to in 1997, the BRA/BIG preference was for a UN force. Having always resisted the BRA's internationalising strategy, the PNG Government also resisted UN peacekeeping. A Truce Monitoring Group (TMG) was established in November 1997, led by Brigadier Roger Mortlock of New Zealand. Half the 250 monitors were New Zealand military, with most of the rest being Australians (civil servants for the front-line roles, where there was distrust of Australian military involvement, though Australian military filled other roles) and military/police from Fiji and Vanuatu. Various informants said there were immediate positive effects from their arrival. Fighters no longer felt they could kill others with impunity. In the newly pacified space, lines of communication began to open up. While the sheer fact of arrival increased confidence that commitments for peace would be kept, the projection of the slogan '*No ken stoppem*[1] *peace*' ('The peace cannot be stopped') by the peace monitors was well crafted to build optimism in the invincibility of the peace.

Both the TMG and subsequent Peace Monitoring Group (PMG) were unarmed. This was driven by BIG/BRA anxiety that Ona and his remaining allies might misinterpret the intentions of an armed intervention—for example, as an Australian invasion to retake the mine. As Anthony Regan (2008) concludes: 'By basing peacekeeping authority on a moral element instead of physical force, it enhances peace by contributing to a non-violent culture.'

In May 1998, the TMG was replaced with a new mission with a similar peacebuilding mandate: the Peace Monitoring Group (PMG). After a softening of initial resistance to Australian leadership, the PMG was led by Australian commanders. There had been successful confidence building through the Australian presence in the TMG. Much of the suspicion about Australian involvement centred on Australian commercial interest in reopening the mine. We were told stories of Australian helicopters 'prospecting for gold' and of Australians being tested with offers to buy gold. The 300-strong PMG was five-sixths Australian (Londey 2004:222) with Australian naval support offshore.

---

1 Sic. It should have been '*stopim*'.

Beyond monitoring the truce, the PMG was to educate citizens about the peace process, provide a framework for the full restoration of government services, oversee the collection and destruction of weapons, foster reconciliation, promote development and help establish a Bougainville police force. PMG commander Osborn saw part of their job as bringing conflicting parties together in dialogue and facilitating negotiations by providing a mixture of 'ideas, information, communication and transport' (Londey 2004:223). The PMG did not provide development aid but helped with medical assistance and transport for locals in response to immediate needs they confronted in the field, while trying to be careful not to distribute favours such as offering rides in ways that seemed to favour one faction over another. The peace operation 'saved many lives, particularly those of mothers and newborn babies'. We interviewed peacekeepers who had babies named after them whom they had helped save by getting their mother to a doctor (sometimes to the concern of their wives!).[2]

Between the deployment of the Truce and Peace Monitoring Groups, the Lincoln peace conference was held in January 1998, bedding down a 'permanent and irrevocable' cease-fire.

In 1997, when the TMG arrived, there could have been 800 PNGDF troops in Bougainville and 150 police mobile fighters armed with automatic weapons within PNGDF patrols (Londey 2004:219). The BRA fighting strength could have been more than 2000 on one account (Londey 2004:219). Anthony Regan's comment on our text here is that the number of core fighters could have been only a couple of hundred, with many more being 'home guards'. The BRA had perhaps 500 automatic weapons and 2000 or 3000 reconditioned World War II or homemade guns (Regan 2001).[3] The Resistance had perhaps 1500 fighters, according to our interviews, though some Resistance leaders claimed 5000 men willing to fight, with a variable number of weapons 'on loan' from the PNGDF. Again, Anthony Regan makes the point that the overwhelming majority of the Resistance forces were little more than home guards.

---

2   One Vanuatu peacekeeper we interviewed was concerned about his wife's reaction to a baby being named after him and the dispatch of gifts to baby and mother in Bougainville. He was relieved when his brother was subsequently posted to Bougainville and able to renew the family connection, reporting back to his brother's wife on the reality of the happy family circumstances of the birth of the baby. Another was greatly relieved to receive a photo of the baby named after him to show his wife how Bougainvillean was the skin colour of the baby!

3   Commenting on these numbers in 2009, Anthony Regan said '[t]hose figures would need to be reconsidered in light of the weapons actually contained from 2001–2005—which were about 2000. The assumption by then was that this might be two-thirds of the total weapons, with perhaps 500 or so still in the hands of the Me'ekamui Defence Force, something similar retained by other elements—BRA/BRF, etc. But we also know there has been some leakage out, some new weapons in, and perhaps 400 or more World War II weapons dug up and brought into circulation.'

Figure 5.1 BRA fighters posing with a US World War II bomber turret gun they had restored

Photo: Brother Bryan Leak

While the TMG was led by New Zealand, it was supported mainly by Australian resources. The Australian Defence Force was an advocate of Australian leadership, but all the diplomatic advice, including from Australia, was that the second-best after UN leadership for BRA acceptance and legitimacy with disarmament would be New Zealand leadership of the TMG. A New Zealand-led regional mission could also be put in place more quickly than a UN-led mission. The UN Security Council lent its support to the operation, but did not open a six-member UN Political Office in Bougainville (UNPOB), with some local employees, until August 1998, after the TMG had handed over to the PMG. Nevertheless, this office of the United Nation's Department of Political Affairs (as opposed to the Department of Peacekeeping Operations) was a central part of the peace process, playing a vital role in bringing the leading parties to the conflict together to discuss the substance and process for the peace.

Ninety per cent of the BRA fighters had followed Kabui and their military commanders, rather than Francis Ona, into the truce. Ona saw the strength of will of the people of Bougainville for peace, which was evident within his own village, and began to adopt the position that he supported peace, but not the particular peace that his former deputies had negotiated. He declared a 'no-go zone' in the mountains centred on his village of Guava and encompassing the mine site. Both the TMG and the PMG respected the no-go zone, hoping that Ona's hold-out force, which became known as the Me'ekamui Defence Force, would eventually fully join the peace and surrender their weapons. Ona almost certainly believed that a peace could not work without him. Instead, he gradually became more marginal and ultimately the Autonomous Bougainville Government and its leadership became more legitimate in the eyes of the people of Bougainville. Bougainvilleans had looked to Ona to get out in front in pushing for peace; his star faded when he failed to hear these hopes.

Outside the no-go zone, the TMG and PMG formed into small patrols that visited most of the villages in Bougainville, explaining the peace process, handing out literature and listening to complaints and concerns. They operated out of five regional centres in addition to the central bases (Regan 2001, 2010:65). The patrols were multinational and each included a woman. The female member of the patrol was important for building rapport with the women of the village. This assisted with maintaining the momentum of women's leadership in peacebuilding. Many of the villages could be reached only on foot. Village meetings often ran for hours. In time, the emphasis shifted from visiting as many villages as possible to spending more time at villages strategic for the peace—for example, where there were a lot of weapons to be handed in or where there were potential spoilers. Peacekeepers learnt the social respect acquired by laying on a feast. They became good at building a relationship over food, with music and through sport[4] (Breen 2001b:48). Even a volleyball team from Francis Ona's village joined in the volleyball competition organised by the PMG; an Australian military surgeon bought them jerseys. Monitors who could play a musical instrument or sing were especially important assets. This leads to some lessons learned from Bougainville: make musical talents a selection criterion for peacekeepers, give singing lessons to interested peacekeepers, and prepare peacekeepers before deployment with some training in how to lay on a feast that indigenes will really appreciate. Australian and New Zealand military commanders saw the peace potential of music and organised several successful tours of Bougainville by military bands.

The Pacific Islander contingents increased more than the diversity of the musicality of the international peacekeepers, though they certainly did that as well:

> I was with a patrol commander, a medic, a civilian monitor and one or two ni-Vanuatu and Fijian peace monitors. They were so much better than we were at picking up the vibe of a village. For example when we would fly in these people could tell us fairly quickly if there had

---

4   Sport, according to some interviews, was especially helpful to the peace when combatants from different sides played on the same team, as opposed to team competitions that mapped onto divides from the conflict.

been something that had happened since the last visit. They had a much quicker rapport with the locals than we did. (Australian peacekeeper interviewed by Reddy 2006:239)

A member of parliament for the Panguna area diagnosed Bougainville's problem as one of distrusting everyone: Papua New Guinea, Australia, but most importantly one another. The TMG/PMG, and particularly the peace newsletter they distributed during their village visits, started to rebuild trust, in his view, by providing factual information that countered some of the wild rumours that were common.

The PMG gradually wound down and finally departed in June 2003. Both the TMG and the PMG were overwhelmingly acclaimed for the sensitive and helpful job they did, though the acclaim for the TMG and for Brigadier Mortlock was even more emphatic than that for the PMG. We consistently failed to draw any criticism during our Bougainville interviews from questions about the biggest mistakes made by peacekeepers or suggestions for how they could have done a better job, though a large number of respondents to the latter question said they should have stayed longer or stayed until all weapons were handed in and until Francis Ona formally joined the peace. There were the occasional allegations of Australians looking for gold from their helicopter and in rivers and another about an Australian soldier smuggling out orchids. This near-universally positive assessment of the monitors was in great contrast with the reaction to peacekeepers we report in the next two Peacebuilding Compared volumes on the Solomon Islands and Timor-Leste and in UN peace operations in other regions. As a top Australian intelligence official said: 'Unlike so many UN operations, there was none of that frequenting of brothels. Monitors were highly disciplined and that was a key to success. New Zealand set a good tone; it worked well because they set good rules early on. [There were] strict rules on fraternisation.'

From July to December 2003, the Bougainville Transitional Team of just 15 remaining from the PMG assisted with the withdrawal of the peacekeepers and the completion of weapons disposal, which still had a long way to go and in 2002 suffered reversals from a number of de-containments of contained weapons in response to perceived or real local threats (UNIFEM 2004). A successor to UNPOB, the UN Observer Mission of Bougainville (UNOMB), continued the UN work in 2004 through to June 2005. All these missions came and went with no casualties from violence. They did leave, however, with perhaps a thousand or more usable weapons not contained.

The post-conflict peace process

Regan (2008) identified three phases to the post-conflict peace process: a process phase that did not attend to outcomes; the negotiated political settlement phase; and the implementation of the settlement phase. The first stage lasted from 1997 to June 1999. It involved establishing the peace process and its institutional architecture, including the Truce and Peace Monitoring Groups and a Peace Process Consultative Committee, a road map for steps towards a negotiated process signed at Lincoln, a 'reconciliation government' 'to unify the Bougainvillean factions in advance of negotiating a political settlement' (Regan 2007), establishing the UN political office in Bougainville (UNPOB) with a mandate to monitor monitors and the peace process more broadly. The Peace Process Consultative Committee, which included no women, was chaired mostly by the director of the UN observer mission. He became in time a more important mediator than the leadership of the Truce and Peace Monitoring Groups of a peace negotiated principally among local leaders. As trust grew, ad hoc meetings of two or more of the parties were also an increasingly important method for settling specific issues (Regan 2005a).

The second phase ran from June 1999 to the signing of the Bougainville Peace Agreement on 30 August 2001. It guaranteed: a referendum on independence for Bougainville, deferred for 10–15 years; a high level of autonomy for Bougainville; and demilitarisation by disposal of the weapons of local combatants and withdrawal of all PNGDF and police mobile forces. The third stage continued from 2001 to the present. It involved real disposal of weapons in a process that continued to 2005 but that left many weapons circulating in Bougainville, especially in the hands of Ona's Me'ekamui Defence Force and Thomas Tari (the commander who captured the weapons at Kangu Beach; Box 4.1). Demand for new weapons from the militarisation of Tonu Village, where Noah Musingku sought refuge, and the realisation that guns could be an export industry for Bougainville criminals have seen in recent years an upsurge in digging up and reconditioning World War II weapons around the old American base in Torokina. In 2009, the US Government finally undertook to clean up the buried weapons it left behind on Bougainville 65 years ago in the interests of the security of the South Pacific (Regan 2010). The third stage of the peace process also involved withdrawal of the PNGDF in 2001, constitutional laws to implement the agreement that were jointly crafted and passed by the PNG Parliament in 2002, a participatory process for drafting a constitution for an Autonomous Bougainville Government (ABG) and an election for the ABG in 2005 that saw Joseph Kabui become President.

Anthony Regan (2010) characterises the peace process as 'political negotiations across two divides'. The first divide separated the Resistance and the BRA. It was in fact a suite of divides along a continuum of positions between strong support for immediate secession and for immediate full integration with Papua New Guinea. The second divide arose after a consensus position among the Bougainville factions was reached. It was between the newly united Bougainville parties and a PNG state that feared even a deferred referendum on independence as a divisive and dangerous precedent.

The first suite of divides was bridged in mid 1999 as Bougainville factions prepared for political negotiations with Papua New Guinea by a process of advisers to all factions jointly developing nine options for the future. These ran from immediate independence to full integration into Papua New Guinea.

Next the advisers assigned tentative ratings to each option—high, medium or low—based on assessments of how well each option could contribute to dealing with the needs of post-conflict Bougainville reflected in 20 criteria (Regan 2002c). These criteria took account of Bougainville's weak economic base and low level of administrative capacity, and so on. This process gave the highest rating to the option of a constitutionally guaranteed referendum on independence for Bougainville from Papua New Guinea combined with a high level of autonomy for Bougainville during the period of deferral. Next, the advisers' analysis was discussed at length by the leadership, who agreed that the highest-rating option provided the best basis for a compromise solution. Only this option balanced the interests of opposing factions by keeping the question of secession alive, but leaving an ultimate decision on the choice between secession and integration to a later democratic process conducted when weapons had been disposed of, reconciliation achieved and the economy restored (Regan 2005a:26–7).

This consensus Bougainvillean negotiating position set the agenda for negotiations with Papua New Guinea that began in June 1999. The PNG negotiating team resisted it fiercely, seeing it as a threat to the unity of the central state that would presage disintegration were it emulated by other provinces. Australian Foreign Minister, Alexander Downer, broke through this deadlock by suggesting the compromise of, first, deferral of a referendum for 10–15 years, and second, substituting the Bougainvillean proposal of a binding referendum with a non-binding referendum subject to the sovereign approval of the PNG Parliament (Wolfers 2002:3). Why would the former BRA leaders agree to a referendum that the PNG Parliament could ignore? Backstage, Downer and the other influential international players persuaded them that the international community could and would pressure Papua New Guinea to honour a vote for independence at that time. Because so much of the PNG budget at that time was funded by Australia, it seemed plausible that this pressure would work. Downer argued that even without that clout over Indonesia, international pressure caused Indonesia to honour the 1999 East Timor independence referendum outcome. This compromise on the Bougainville compromise finally crossed Regan's two divides. Minister for Bougainville Affairs, Moi Avei—as Peter Barter had done—built a high degree of trust with the Bougainvillean and PNG players at this critical moment (Regan 2002b:118).

The other key part of the agreement was that the Autonomous Government of Bougainville would have full authority to administer its own affairs, to legislate across the entire gamut of governance, including those areas most embroiled in the conflict: land, minerals and other natural resources and the environment. Key exceptions reserved for the central government were most foreign affairs and defence powers, central banking, international trade, customs and quarantine, international shipping and civil aviation, industrial relations and posts and telecommunications. Bougainville would have its own police, courts and taxation power.

The next priority was drafting a *Constitution of the Autonomous Region of Bougainville*. The draft was completed between 2002 and 2004 by a 24-member Bougainville Constitutional Commission that was broadly representative. The constitution was discussed, amended and ultimately adopted in November 2004 by a broadly based Bougainville Constituent Assembly.

Credible commitment architecture

As we have documented, Papua New Guinea and Bougainville had a history of deep distrust. Yet Papua New Guinea did have a comparatively good record of credibly committed constitutionalism. So the Bougainville negotiators derived assurance from entrenching the commitment to a referendum in the *PNG Constitution*. Double entrenchment was accomplished by requiring consent of the Bougainville legislature for any constitutional amendment relating to Bougainville (Wolfers 2006a). Even more creative was the embedding of implementation assurance in an architecture of 'sequencing of, and linkages between, agreed-upon steps for implementation of key arrangements' (Regan 2008). Each side committed to steps where it yielded up some power, provided the other gave it some power first. One party's stepwise commitment was a precondition for the step-by-step commitments of the other.

The main linkages are between the provisions, on the one hand, for disposal of weapons by Bougainvillean factions and, on the other hand, the withdrawal of PNG forces from Bougainville and, more importantly, the constitutionalising and implementation of the agreed arrangements. The linkages involved completion of steps agreed to by one party being specified as a 'condition precedent' to be completed before the other party was required to take a separate step. In particular, the obligation on Bougainville's ex-combatant groups to move weapons to secure storage arose only on Papua New Guinea both making the constitutional amendments implementing the agreement and beginning the withdrawal of its forces from Bougainville. In order to maintain pressure on Bougainvillean groups to dispose of their weapons, after the constitutional amendments implementing the agreement were passed by Parliament, they did not come into operation until the UN mission verified completion of stage two of weapons disposal (secure containment). Lack of substantial compliance with the agreed-on weapons disposal process could have resulted in the UN mission delaying elections for the ABG (any party to the agreement could call on the United Nations to verify and certify substantial compliance with weapons disposal and whether the level of security for the weapons was conducive to the holding of elections) (Regan 2008).

There is contextual genius in this architecture that gives parties who have taken pride in tricking one another incentives to honour their commitments. The sequencing has proceeded not always punctiliously and punctually, but pretty well. Particularly slow has been the transfer of specific governance competencies to the Bougainville administration (for a discussion of notice and other procedures for transfer, see Wolfers 2008). The Bougainville civil servants so far remain much more under the authority of their civil service bosses in Port Moresby than Bougainville ministers and the ABG President. This is partly a matter of Bougainville politicians needing time to develop experience in directing civil servants. Bougainville does not yet have its own court system; its judicial branch is part of the PNG judiciary. Capacity bottlenecks are the main reason why so few executive and judicial competencies have shifted to Bougainville so far. There is just so much to be done with building the full range of state capacities from scratch in such a small polity. In all areas, state capacity in Bougainville remains stunted. International assistance for this work has been less than it should have been—strikingly less than we will encounter in our next case study, the Solomon Islands.

The positive side of this is that Bougainvilleans are taking their time to construct their own autonomy in their own way. For Anthony Regan (2005a:44), this is part of the virtue of 'extended timetables with which managers of international interventions are usually not comfortable'.[5] In the Regan view, improved state capacity that comes slowly in response to local pressure for better service for

---

5 This does not have to be inconsistent with moments when pushing through to a result for a negotiation deadline through a kind of exhaustion has no place. Brigadier Osborn (2001:52) described the negotiations the night before the scheduled cease-fire signing ceremony of 30 April 1998: 'The signatories and the TMG had only agreed on its contents at 3.50 am that morning on *HMAS Tobruk*.' Dr Bob Breen, who was on the *Tobruk*, said that the women leaders played a vital role that night and morning as go-betweens and in pushing the men to the point where they would sign. When we asked Breen to check if we had got this right, he contacted two other senior Australians who were on the *Tobruk*, one of whom 'was adamant that the women shamed the men into signing the implementing agreement', with the other 'supporting this view'. The women had also played important goading and go-between roles at Burnham and Lincoln before the male leaders were ready to join hands. And they had often done that before in the jungles where battles were being fought.

citizens is more likely to be sustained and more genuinely responsive to needs as well. There remains a worry that the sequencing of commitments of the peace might work well up to the last step. To be blunt—and hopefully unfair—we fear there was good reason for Bougainville to be distrustful of the PNG state. If Bougainville votes for independence in a few years, will the PNG Parliament vote to honour their choice? Our interviews suggest many in the current PNG Parliament would not. There is much persuasive diplomatic work to be done by the many—nationally and internationally—who believe independence is not in the interests of economic and human development for Bougainvilleans. They need to get on with that conversation with the people of Bougainville just as they need to engage the present and potential future leaders of Papua New Guinea with the need—in the interests of such a hard-won peace—for national and international resolve to honour whatever the people of Bougainville decide is best for them.

The peace that was won in Bougainville was remarkable. Many experienced hardheads who were close to the action did not believe it could hold. The architecture of sequenced, linked commitments described above deserves some of the credit for it holding so far. If it does unravel in a final fateful feat of betrayal of Bougainville, we should not throw out the lesson that has *already* been learned about the contribution contextually attuned linked sequencing of commitments can make to peace. This is not to say that the particular sequencing that has secured 12 years of peace in Bougainville will work elsewhere. In most contexts, it would be wildly imprudent to delay weapons destruction for as long as it was delayed in Bougainville—just as having unarmed peacekeepers would often be a naive step in other circumstances. In Aceh (Braithwaite et al. 2010:Ch. 6), we saw that peacemaking failed when it opted for a truce deferring a political settlement and weapons destruction until confidence building proceeded; yet peacemaking succeeded in Aceh when a 'nothing is agreed until everything is agreed' political settlement preceded the cease-fire. What we laud in this book is the contextually attuned architecture of linkages that in this particular case saw the truce precede the political settlement. This is not to laud its specific sequence as generally applicable. We know that failures of credible commitment recurrently explain the outbreak of war (Collier et al. 2003). We know that peacemakers can learn to 'think in time' (Neustadt and May 1986) by asking contextual questions.

Disarming Bougainville

The Bougainville peace process was unusual in that the international peace monitors departed long before weapons disposal was completed. The PMG also made no real attempt to disarm the Me'ekamui Defence Force though elements of the force broke away and joined in, disposing of their weapons (Wolfers 2006b:7), as the peace process progressed. Francis Ona seemed to have no intention of an armed assault to take over Bougainville. He knew that the people of Bougainville would not support that—nor would many of his former fighters. When we asked a group of Resistance commanders what they would have done if Ona had sought to use his guns to re-conquer Bougainville, one said, 'Our guns were in boxes, but we had keys.' When we quibbled, pointing out that the United Nations held the second key, he said, 'We had bolt-cutters too.'

Figure 5.2 BRA fighters, 1994, with homemade weapons and a World War II Japanese canon reconditioned at the Panguna mine workshops

Photo: Ben Bohane

Ona was a hold-out, as he saw it, because it was only a matter of time before the people of Bougainville would come to his view that the truce was a trick. Papua New Guinea would betray Bougainville and then the people would come back to him. There were some in the BRA who went with the peace thinking that if Ona was right after all, it would perhaps be as well that Ona was holding out with his guns in the no-go zone. Sam Kauona (2001:88) went close to saying this even in 2001: 'We would rather he join us in the peace process, but in a way Francis provides the check and balance by staying out. He serves as a warning; as a reminder of the alternative if the peace process fails.' It is still quite possible that Papua New Guinea will not honour its commitment to defer to the people of Bougainville if they vote for independence a few years from now. In 2005, Ona died without being vindicated. The Me'ekamui Defence Force, however, lives on. At different times since Ona's death, different individuals—including Noah Musingku and Chris Uma—have claimed to have inherited Ona's control of the force and its weapons. Some local informants said in 2007 that after Musingku had broken away to form with Fijian-trained fighters a different node of opposition to the ABG, there remained three factions of the old Me'ekamui Defence Force. One was the faction led by Uma, another was a group loyal to Ona and the third was a group who had been suspended from the Me'ekamui Defence Force by Ona for criticising his collaborations with certain white people. In early 2010, some unity has formed among many of the Me'ekamui factions, particularly in the no-go zone, joining together in the new peace processes led by President Tanis, but fragmentation remains or has increased around Noah Musingku and possibly Chris Uma.

The reality of Me'ekamui hold-outs has created an unstable situation in southern Bougainville in recent years. The considerable residual access to automatic weapons in the south has played into a variety of historical grievances between different groups and families, different armed factions from the war and into opportunities to exploit greed through roadblocks, extortion from the government and other criminal activities. A new push on weapons disposal is needed and President Tanis has been seeking to secure agreement to this. His successor, John Momis, promised during his 2010 election campaign that he would continue this push. Getting the agreement of the US Government to clean up its World War II weapons has been an encouraging start. A good example of the problem is the conflict between the Damien Koike and Thomas Tari groups, which have each been responsible for killings of members of the other group, with Koike attempting to kill Tari and Tari attempting to kill Koike. It was an inter-family, inter-warlord struggle for control in which each used the continued access to the formidable arsenals of the other to justify their own refusal to destroy weapons.

In 2001, when progress was stalling on the weapons disposal process, Australia provided A$5 million for small income-generating projects for ex-combatant groups in communities where weapons disposal was proceeding. Combatants were also promised amnesties and pardons for conflict-related offences as part of the 2001 peace deal. The three stages of the agreed weapons disposal process were completed only in May 2005 (Regan 2005a). This involved collecting weapons into locked boxes that were regularly audited by the PMG (Spark and Bailey 2005:601). At first, ex-combatant commanders of the units that surrendered the weapons kept the keys. In the second stage, locally contained weapons were consolidated into more centrally located double-locked containers. The UN observer mission held the second key. After UN verification of completion of the second stage, the third stage was final disposal/destruction of the weapons.

Seven and a half years between truce and disposal of (perhaps most) weapons was a long and risky wait. In fact, it was a double-edged risk. One side of that risk was what Thomas Tari did: refusing to dispose of the weapons at the end of the agreed containment stage, and later breaking open the containers and creating a certain amount of havoc with them as a post-conflict criminal entrepreneur. Another was the larger risk of restarting the war, which did not happen. But the biggest risk of that happening was posed by the Me'ekamui Defence Force, which was not a party to the peace or to weapons containment. The BRA and Resistance could only credibly promise to protect the unarmed international peace monitors because in the circumstances of an attack on them by the Me'ekamui Defence Force they could open the containers.

Anthony Regan's (2010) most recent update—headed for press at the time of writing—suggests that the weapons retained by the Me'ekamui Defence Force (MDF) could have been much greater than previously believed:

> It was estimated by senior BRA figures at the time that the MDF held about 400 to 500 weapons, though more recent estimates by former BRA and MDF leaders who, since 2009, have been seeking to facilitate development of a weapons disposal process involving the MDF elements in the former 'no-go-zone' in the vicinity of the Panguna mine…suggest that there could be a much greater number of weapons in the hands of MDF elements—perhaps as many as 2,500 (including a substantial, though as yet unknown, number of WWII weapons as well as significant amounts of ammunition from the former US/Australian World War II base at Torokina, most obtained since 2005). (Regan 2010)

Credible commitment and confidence in the peace

Delayed, graduated and partial weapons disposal linked to constitutionalisation of autonomy and a referendum provided a unique panoply of assurances. It would begin and progress only after the political settlement and constitutional changes began and ended (and after the PNGDF had completely departed). And it remained in place until the year of Francis Ona's death—seemingly from natural causes. Stages of disarmament did not proceed until stages of politico-legal transition and stages of marginalisation of Francis Ona were behind the wary factions. By May 2005, 1900 weapons had been destroyed and UNOMB certified that stage three of the disposal process was complete and the community was now living with a sense of security. Some police think it could be accurate that two-thirds of all weapons that had been circulating have been contained, but the figure is considerably less than that for factory-made weapons. Thomas

Tari's arsenal (Box 6.1), which had been part of the peace process, and the Me'ekamui Defence Force arsenal, which was beyond the reach of the peace process, were significant on their own. Many weapons were also sold to be used in fighting in the New Guinea Highlands and in the conflict in the Solomon Islands (Alpers 2005:65, 69). Philip Alpers (2005:41) reports that two of the F-1 machine guns that Australia shipped to Papua New Guinea for use in the Bougainville war were seized by Southern Highlands Police in Wogia. National Intelligence Organisation officers in 2007 reported they still regularly received reports of the movement of guns into and out of Bougainville. It was far from a perfect weapons destruction process. Weapons destruction after war never works perfectly. In Bougainville, it worked credibly enough to consolidate peace but not well enough to give Bougainvilleans security from former BRA commanders who became minor post-conflict criminal entrepreneurs such as Thomas Tari, Damien Koike and Chris Uma, and indeed from Noah Musingku.

Yet it might have been better if the PMG had stayed at least until Thomas Tari, the Me'ekamui Defence Force and Damien Koike's group were fully disarmed and all roadblocks that secured no-go zones with guns were dismantled. That might have been done with a patient winding down of the size of the commitment of personnel to quite a minimal level, but with a willingness to escalate—and indeed escalate to armed peacekeeping—had diplomacy at the roadblocks failed through the reality or the promise of armed violence. Volker Boege and Edward Wolfers both questioned in their comments on this conclusion whether it ever had been or would be necessary to mobilise for armed enforcement. Wolfers said: 'The progress made in encouraging former hold-outs to engage in the peace process, including efforts by former President Joseph Kabui shortly before he died,[6] and by his successor, James Tanis, would seem to belie the arguments for a delayed peace process or possible international armed intervention.' Further progress in broadening the genuine engagement of various hold-out armed factions, with courageous support from church, chiefly and other traditional leaders, including many women who walked into armed camps to talk peace, in the six months after Wolfers' comments would seem to vindicate his analysis. This steady expansion of the peace certainly does caution against any hasty resort to peace enforcement or police enforcement by making the point that patient local diplomacy has slowly born fruit.

---

6   The *Panguna Communiqué*, signed at a large reconciliation meeting in August 2007 (Boege 2008:11; Wolfers 2008:189), was the culmination of a process of discussion by President Kabui and leaders of his government with Me'ekamui leaders in the preceding months. It greatly expanded the path for the restoration of government services to the no-go zone and the dismantling of roadblocks. Included as a minor part of this process was a two-day peacemaking conference organised by the Peacebuilding Compared Project, the Buka Open Campus of the University of Papua New Guinea and the ABG, attended by the President and by James Tanis throughout and also by Me'ekamui leaders on the occasion of the second anniversary of the ABG in June 2007. Willie Aga signed this communiqué on behalf of the Me'ekamui Defence Force. A video of this entire conference can be found on the Peacebuilding Compared web site.

While the top-down architecture of the peace we have described in this chapter has been critical to the peace that has been secured so far, an even more important ingredient is the bottom-up reconciliation and reintegration discussed in the next chapter. Yet a central conclusion of this book will be that this is a peace with a mutually enabling relationship between a top-down credible commitment architecture and bottom-up reconciliation.

6. Reconciliation and reintegration

Reconciliation

Local reconciliation efforts began 'almost as soon as the conflict began' (Regan 2005a:15), gathered momentum throughout the 1990s and continued at the time of writing. There has long been recognition in Bougainville that reconciliation takes decades rather than years. In some areas, reconciliation processes following intertribal fighting occasioned by World War II continued into the 1980s (Londey 2004:224; Nelson 2005:196).

Every village-level story of reconciliation was unique. The village where John Braithwaite lived in 1969 had been the base of C Company of the BRA. In 1991, they had been involved in assaults on the PNGDF at Buka after swimming across Buka Passage with their weapons. A PNGDF patrol-boat supplied by Australia had fired on the village. Starting in 1990, when the war became chaotic, voices in the village began to be raised in favour of adopting a position of neutrality. Women from across Selau organised a peace march followed by an all-night vigil for peace that it is claimed 5000 attended—most of the population of Selau (van Tongeren et al. 2005:124). The war had opened up some old internal divisions. There were allegations that the local BRA commander had used his position to murder a man who was much disapproved of because of sorcery. He was also fearfully reviled by many because he had married his own daughter. In turn, there were allegations that the combat death of that local BRA commander was 'friendly fire', which was in fact 'unfriendly fire' from loyal kin of the murdered sorcerer within C Company. Others dispute this. Reconciliation within the area and between the PNGDF and the village was accomplished in August 1991 after the women seized the peacemaking agenda with the council of chiefs and the village declared itself neutral (Saovana-Spriggs 2007:195).

Both the villagers and the PNGDF officer who attended the reconciliation ceremony remember it as moving and a turning point towards local peace. It was a peace that created an island of civility (Kaldor 1999)—a peace zone—in the Selau region, which demonstrated the advantages of peaceful neutrality to those living in adjacent conflict areas, in a similar way that the North Nasioi peace zone did after 1994 in Central Bougainville. The PNGDF loaded all the BRA weapons from that part of Selau onto a helicopter and Sister Lorraine Garasu and elder Bernadette Ropa dropped them into the deep water just offshore from the village as part of the ceremony. This sealed the peace and the weapons disposal in this little corner of Bougainville many years before the peacekeepers of the Truce and Peace Monitoring Groups arrived. The story of such a single village reveals why we must always be circumspect with the grand narrative of the Bougainville peace that says it was negotiated at Burnham and Lincoln. It was in fact a cumulative peace that took quantum leaps at Burnham and Lincoln, but was still an incomplete peace even at the time of writing for those who lived in the persisting no-go zones of different factions of the Me'ekamui Defence Force. Some PNG security forces personnel who attended reconciliations such as that in Selau reported them as the most positive memories of their time in Bougainville, saying that the aspect of the ceremonies that most moved them was when both the soldiers and the villagers had the opportunity to speak about their personal feelings of loss for particular individuals who had fallen. One of these officers said Bougainvillean women peacemakers changed him as a soldier:

> I was a very aggressive traditional soldier. Very tough on people. As a result of my experience on Bougainville, I changed. I listen to my soldiers more now. I think negotiation is more important. [He explained how he was particularly affected by the compassion of women with children who had lost their husbands]…I wonder if my own wife would react that way if it was me who was killed. (PNGDF interview, Port Moresby 2007)

The Selau region has a population of only 7000, but the chiefs told us in April 2006 that they had participated in 87 separate formal reconciliations by then. While hundreds of large reconciliations have been held across Bougainville for big groups, and thousands of smaller ones in relation to hamlets, families or individuals, a widespread perspective a decade after the war is that most of the reconciliations that are needed still remain to be done.

The peace in Bougainville is two stories. There is the story of top-down peace ultimately negotiated under New Zealand auspices in 1997 and 1998, and ultimately under UN facilitation of the political settlement between PNG and Bougainvillean factions in 1999, 2000 and 2001. And there is the story of zones of local reconciliation (see Boege 2006:11) starting soon after the onset of war and continuing the struggle to expand its reach two decades later. The continuation of this story into the late 2000s is well illustrated by the large spike of reconciliations associated with the Youth Cross (Box 6.1). Most accounts assume the top-down story is the master narrative and the bottom-up reconciliations are subsidiary. But in important ways the bottom-up micro-narratives subsume and infuse the top-down peace. This way of thinking—that peacebuilding starts in families and ripples out from there—was repeatedly emphasised in our conversations with Bougainvilleans (Tanis 2002b).[1] In that way of thinking about the peace, the 'failed' Arawa peace of 1994 that led to the Miriung vision of the North Nasioi peace zone and a transitional government that empowered chiefs, women, church and youth leaders to lead local reconciliations under councils of elders is an intermediate narrative that infuses the master peace narrative. It laid the foundation, for example, for 700 women to come together again in Arawa in 1996 to assign specific peacebuilding objectives to women leaders from every corner of Bougainville (Rolfe 2001:51). This was supported by the Uniting Church in Australia (Eagles 2002). Peter Reddy's (2006) PhD thesis, moreover, shows that just as Bougainville is not a master narrative of successful peacebuilding, Somalia is not a master narrative of failed peacebuilding. He read Bougainville as a story of successful peacebuilding in three-quarters of Bougainville and (at that time) failed peacebuilding in one-quarter (the no-go zones), while Somalia was the reverse: a failed peace in three-quarters of the nation and a flourishing peace in one-quarter (Somaliland).

Box 6.1 The Youth Cross

We have seen that one of the strengths of peacebuilding in Bougainville is the Church. And a strength of the international peacekeeping was that it worked this strength by giving its three chaplains—'The Three Amigos'—free rein to work the churches as a central plank of its peacebuilding strategy. It was the Church that gave the most important base to the peacebuilding work of the women. The Youth Cross story is about how in the post-post-conflict period it gave an organisational base to youth leaders who wanted to take reconciliation to a new level. The Youth Cross story also shows that while the big story of reconciliation in Bougainville is about indigenous traditions of peacemaking, almost as big a story is the grafting of Christian traditions of healing onto the peace process.

World Youth Day—a huge gathering of Catholic young people—was held in Sydney in 2008. A lead-up in 2007 was the Youth Cross travelling to many countries of the world on its way to Sydney. The Youth Cross came to Papua New Guinea, but to the dismay of Catholic youth in Bougainville, not to their island. So the youth of Bougainville made their own little cross, travelled to Rabaul to place it on the Youth Cross, then placed it on their own large wooden cross back in Bougainville.

---

1   More widely, Bougainville looks like a case where social capital (trust building as well as peacebuilding) ripples out from local accomplishments (Job and Reinhart 2003). We thought of this after attending a ceremony for the arrival of a large number of water tanks in a Siwai village. The paramount chief said: 'This is no small thing we have done together. What a great leader we have found in the chairman we appointed for this water tank project. And what a great committee he had working with him. Look what we have accomplished here.'

The Catholic Youth of Bougainville decided that the theme for the visits of the Youth Cross would be 'peace and reconciliation'. The youth believed they could show their elders how their generation could take reconciliation up to a new and more spiritual level. While it was a Catholic event, the Protestant churches were all invited to join in, which they did when they saw what a huge following the cross was attracting to Siwai. During our 2007 fieldwork, we followed the Youth Cross from Siwai into Bana District. For much of its journey, the cross was followed by thousands of people. Days of fasting and prayer preceded its arrival in most villages. At that point, it was stopping at every village for three days and we were told that the plan was that it would stop in every village in Bougainville. It should have been clear that there was not time to accomplish this before World Youth Day 2008. And in any case, we are told that the enormous ecumenical momentum we saw the Youth Cross to have in Siwai waned as some Protestant communities further north took offence at some of the iconography of preparing roadsides for the arrival of the cross.

Miracles occurred as the cross moved from village to village and some who were the subject of the miracles then became celebrities following the cross around the island. For example, one man, a village drunk, cursed at the cross when it entered his village. He instantly dropped dead. Half an hour later, miraculously, he returned to life. While he was dead, he saw many wonderful things, met many long-dead ancestors and was able to report messages from them to the crowd.

At all of the dozen villages about which we made inquiries in south-western Bougainville, major reconciliations in front of the cross relating to the nine-year civil war occurred. A Catholic priest told us that in Siwai alone, 500 separate war-related reconciliations had occurred in front of the cross. Unfortunately, he said these did not touch the remaining really major conflicts in Siwai. Reconciliation did occur, however, between the police and Noah Musingku's Palace Guards over the 2006 fire fight at the 'Royal Palace' and it was said this paved the way for opening the roadblock on the road to Tonu.

Some reconciliations related to killings, rapes and other serious crimes, where the perpetrator(s) went before the cross as it stood in the village to ask forgiveness from the victim or their family. Many were groups who went before the cross asking forgiveness from their victims. One of these (see Figure 6.1) involved a young Me'ekamui fighter and raskol who had robbed a micro-finance bank with a gun that he cut in half in front of the cross. During the robbery, shots were fired and a stray bullet hit a young mother with a baby. During negotiations in the days before the cross arrived in the young man's village, the local police sergeant gave the young man a '100 per cent guarantee' that he would not be prosecuted if he asked for forgiveness from the mother in front of the cross and changed his ways. We asked the sergeant if anyone in the community criticised him for not prosecuting such a serious crime. No, he said, everyone in the community thought it was the right thing to do and everyone felt safer when a young raskol destroyed his gun and committed to obey the law in a spiritually profound reconciliation like this.

Rarely was monetary compensation paid in the reconciliations that occurred before the Youth Cross. The cross arrived in a village in the late afternoon and reconciliations occurred right through the night into the next day. It must have been exhausting (but exhilarating too) for the local priest. In Siwai, awe-struck children sat closest to the cross under cover, with the adult audience standing at the back in the sun.

The celebrations before the cross were theologically interesting. As a priest scowled at John Braithwaite, he said that some people would have us believe that Jesus was a waitman, when in fact Jesus was born in Nagovis. In some villages, when the time came for the procession of the cross to move down the road to the next village, those who would lift the cross from its base announced that it was stuck. 'The cross is stuck', reverberated around the gathering. 'Someone must step forward to ask forgiveness before the cross leaves.' And someone would step forward, finally finding the courage to ask for forgiveness.

This was a very different reconciliation context than the traditional one. The short time frame between the impending arrival of the cross and the proposed reconciliation before the crisis gave victims little time to come to terms with the reconciliation on big matters. One of our neighbours in Siwai was told by a former BRA commander as the cross was approaching the village that he had killed her husband and he pleaded for forgiveness before the cross. She had no idea that this man had killed her husband. It was a lot to digest, yet it was a successful reconciliation that moved the whole community. But in other such cases the cross moved on to the next village with the parties still working on the healing process through planned future reconciliation meetings.

John Paul Lederach (1997) influentially argued that peace must be not only top-down and bottom-up, but also middle-out. Bottom-up connects the grassroots to the political projects of elites; top-down connects capacities that can be mobilised only by national elites down to lower levels of the society. Middle-out complements these vertical capacities with horizontal capacities to move back and forth across social divides. Organisations in civil society that are intermediate between the state and families/hamlets often do this middle-out work. Yet in his more recent book, Lederach finds a web metaphor more useful.

What he calls the middle-out capacity is in fact strategic networking that 'creates a web of relationships and activities that cover the setting' (Lederach 2005:80). The women of Bougainville certainly did this with peace marches that wound across the island, connecting new women to the network at each hamlet they passed (Ninnes 2006). So did the next generation of youth with the journeys of the Youth Cross. Lederach (2005:91) perceptively sees the key to weaving these webs as 'getting a small set of the right people involved at the right places. What's missing is not the critical mass. The missing ingredient is the *critical yeast*.'

In Bougainville, women such as Sister Lorraine Garasu were that yeast and many local male peacemakers were as well. Gradually enough yeast is connected to the project of building the bread of peace and the mass of the bread rises. Lederach (2005:90) connects this to Malcolm Gladwell's (2002) idea from marketing of *The Tipping Point*. Gladwell's subtitle is 'How little things make a difference'. The Bougainville peace is a classic illustration of how little peacemakers finally linked together to tip momentum towards peace to a critical mass. This happened even as top-down peacemakers such as Theodore Miriung and John Bika were assassinated and even as the leaders of the war (Ona and the PNGDF) remained spoilers of sorts,[2] and even as profit-seeking international spoilers (Sandline and the shadowy multinational mining interests backing them) butted in. Once the tipping point of bottom-up support for peace was passed, progressive elements in the BRA and in the PNG military and political elite moved around the spoilers to join hands with the Sister Lorraines and the great mass of Bougainvillean peacemakers they had leavened. Gradually more elements of the Me'ekamui Defence Force right up to the time of writing in 2009 have joined in reconciliations and joined the peace.

While reconciliation of the more traditional kind, as opposed to the religious kind such as we see with the Youth Cross, is transacted in somewhat different ways in different parts of Bougainville, reciprocal gift giving by the two sides to a conflict that is intended to restore balance and social harmony is universal (Regan 2010). Pigs and ceremonial shell money are mostly the gifts involved and often small amounts of cash, which are not intended as reparation but as symbols of sorrow for the spilt blood. While the commercialisation of reconciliations by demanding large amounts of cash as reparation is not the widespread problem of 'manipulation of custom' (Fraenkel 2004) that it is in the Solomon Islands, it

---

2   While at the time of the assassination of Bika, it seems accurate to call Ona a spoiler, Edward Wolfers makes the thoughtful point in a comment on this paragraph that at later stages Ona became more an absentee than a spoiler: 'While Ona remained a determined hold-out, he was not a "spoiler" of the peace process overall. He did not, on the whole, try to disrupt what others were doing. The parties' willingness to keep moving ahead, combined with the national government's repeated invitation to Ona and the Me'ekamui Defence Force to join in the peace process, meant that they were absentees rather than "spoilers".'

is a worry in Bougainville that such demands have arisen in many cases. Patrick Howley of the Peace Foundation Melanesia has articulated the view of many concerned Bougainvilleans:

> To the outsider the gift may seem to be compensation (blood money). However, to most Bougainvilleans compensation (blood money) is repugnant. A gift is to wash away the tears; it in no way is a payment for the loss incurred. Compensation is for gain and is equivalent to setting a value on the life of a loved one. With a gift, one asks for forgiveness; with compensation there is no forgiveness and the person is attempting something which is impossible, that is putting a value on something that cannot be bought or paid for. With our experience (Peace Foundation), we have decided that if people want money for compensation (blood money), then we refuse to mediate and tell them to take it to the court... Not only does the blood money fail to produce reconciliation but it also leads to further disputes and fighting. (Howley n.d.)

In a small number of cases, post-conflict reconciliations have included an exchange of young women to marry into the enemy group, using kinship bonds to consolidate the peace. Traditionally, this was a widespread element of reconciliation. With the near-complete demise of arranged marriages as the norm in Bougainville, however, we have seen this particular form of arranged marriage also disappearing. At a reconciliation meeting we attended in Buka, one of the older men argued this was the only way to reconsolidate bonds deeply between the two groups; a few people sniggered, some smiled at each other at such an impractical, backward-looking suggestion, some frowned and most ignored it. Betel-nut is usually shared and chewed together as a ritual of greeting among friends or introduction of strangers. There is singing and dancing. In some cases, return of the bones of a person killed in the conflict is the most important exchange. A rock may be buried or a tree planted to symbolise permanency of the peace, the growing, restored relationships and a weight that is put away forever; spears, bows and arrows may be broken. Our interviews (like Reddy's 2006:246) testified to the ethos of permanence with reconciliations, though there were suggestions that in the south reconciliations could be less irrevocable than in the traditions of central and northern Bougainville. The weight of social disapproval from renouncing a reconciliation was reported to be enormous. 'The moment the hatchet is buried, it stays buried. Anyone seen to be digging up the buried hatchet will get the most severe punishment. This means death' (Interview with President Kabui, ABG, 2006).

Figure 6.1a: Young women lead the Youth Cross as it arrives from one village into another.

Figure 6.1b: Young men with panpipes kneeling behind thousands following the Youth Cross as it travels from one Siwai village to another.

Figure 6.1c: A young Me'ekamui fighter surrenders a reconditioned World War II weapon to be cut in two in front of the Youth Cross and is forgiven in Siwai. He recently shot a woman in an armed robbery and this reconciliation became a catalyst for opening a roadblock on the road to Tonu village and for local police–Me'ekamui reconciliation

Photos: Anonymous Siwai photographer or John Braithwaite, 2007

Tarout or vomiting—as discussed earlier in the description of the Burnham peace talks—often occurs as part of the whole process, though usually at the preparatory meetings where what will be exchanged is hammered out. A long sequence of mediation meetings between dozens of chiefs builds up to a public reconciliation ceremony that hundreds, even thousands in rare cases, might attend. This is why this form of peacebuilding is at the heart of the highly participative peace accomplished in Bougainville. At the large final ceremony, both sides express concerns and remorse. Apologies by men are often tearful and can be responded to with tearful, loud, demonstrative displays of sadness and very often forgiveness by the women who are the closest family to the victims who are subjects of the apology. Christian traditions of prayers of solace and pleas for forgiveness are normally intertwined with the indigenous traditions of the reconciliation ritual. Both their indigenous origins and their Christian elements gave this path to peace special legitimacy in the eyes of Bougainvilleans (Regan 2005a). 'Women's leaders and groups also initiated many such efforts, often drawing on long-established traditional dispute-settlement roles of women' (Regan 2005a:16). The sheer spread of such local reconciliations put 'pressure on leaders of all Bougainville factions' (Regan 2005a:17), including Francis Ona and other potential spoilers, not to unsettle the peace.

Dr Bob Breen, who is writing the official Australian history of peacekeeping in Bougainville, and who served as a senior military advisor to the Australian commanders in Bougainville, thinks the greatest contribution of the peacekeepers was in accelerating reconciliations that would have eventually occurred naturally. That is, one of the hardest things with starting a reconciliation for inter-group killings is for someone to take the risk of proposing a meeting. According to Breen, this was the most valuable single thing peacekeepers did: simply going to one group and suggesting that it would be good if they met with another with a view to making peace locally—and offering to be in attendance to provide a kind of third-party security guarantee for the risky meeting. Australian and New Zealand peacekeepers particularly learnt from ni-Vanuatu peacekeepers how to set up a meeting in a patient Melanesian way.

There are two sides to traditional Bougainvillean reconciliations. On the one hand, there is the commitment to rituals of forgiveness that puts revenge aside (usually permanently). On the other hand, when a person becomes a recurrent potential spoiler of the peace—particularly when they flout a reconciliation agreement of which they are a part—a much less frequently used aspect of traditional Bougainvillean social control is for their relatives to kill them (by surprising them on a hunting trip, for example). Many informants agreed that in the Bougainville peace process, more than a few spoilers on both sides were killed by their own kin to preserve the peace—perhaps as many as 10.

During 2009, when this book was being written, major new reconciliations occurred. One was between local commanders of the Me'ekamui Defence Force and the Wisai Liberation Movement (WILMO) in May 2009. Another was held in Tonu between BRA Buin commander, Thomas Tari, and Me'ekamui Defence Force southern commander, Damien Koike—according to one report, with 3000 people in attendance. This reconciliation also encompassed the attack Tari led on Noah Musingku's U-Vistract headquarters at Tonu in 2006. A major reconciliation between the PNGDF and the people of Buin over the Kangu Beach massacre was also at an advanced stage of planning. In June 2009, Sir Julius Chan, supported by the whole cabinet of his New Ireland Province, and traditional culture groups participated in reconciliation ceremonies all day on 13 June at which Sir Julius apologised for his role with Sandline. The festivities continued with his group's participation in the fourth anniversary of the Autonomous Bougainville Government on 15 June 2009. During 2009, ABG President, James Tanis, energised yet another wave of important reconciliations with different Me'ekamui factions and other armed factions in the south, including Noah Musing'ku, with whom amnesty was discussed during 2009.

Figure 6.2 Bougainville President, James Tanis, washes the feet of former PNG Prime Minister Sir Julius Chan during their 2009 reconciliation

Photo: Aloysius Laukai, New Dawn

Restorative justice and the new Bougainville justice system

There is a desire in Bougainville to develop a criminal justice system different from the one seen in the retributive behaviour of the PNG riot police that was a cause of the war. The *Report of the Bougainville Constitutional Commission* makes numerous specific references to shifting away from the PNG criminal justice system and towards restorative justice (Reddy 2006:249). One of the most prominent restorative justice advocates on Bougainville—whom our ethics policies prohibit us from naming—ordered his BRA unit to destroy Bougainville's only prison. Today he works at trying to rebuild the Bougainville criminal justice system from the ground up as a more restorative system. Almost two decades on from the burning of the prison, Bougainville still does not have a jail. It is not high on Bougainville's long list of state-building priorities, though it is on the list. Australia has been pushing for it to be higher and is offering to fund a new prison. Bougainville respondents to the National Research Institute

(2005:47) survey rarely rated 'harsher penalties from the courts' as one of the 'government initiatives to make your area safer from crime'. Their priorities in response to this were, in descending order: youth activities, more jobs, more police, better living conditions and fighting corruption. There are human rights problems with crowded police lock-ups, though most detainees are free to roam the vicinity of the lock-up during the day and eat meals with their relatives.

While the *PNG Constitution* provides for a 'Police Force', the *Bougainville Constitution* provides for a 'Police Service' that will 'develop rehabilitatory and reconciliatory concepts of policing', 'work in harmony with communities and encourage community participation in its activities' and 'support and work with traditional chiefs...to resolve disputes' (Regan 2005a:40). We attended high-quality restorative justice training for the police provided by the Peace Foundation Melanesia. Scheye and Peake (2005:258–9) contend that the war created an opportunity for chiefs to deputise community members as what Dinnen and Braithwaite (2009) might prefer to conceive as more like indigenous *kiaps* than police. Post-conflict, Scheye and Peake contend the writers of the new Bougainville constitution had the wisdom to deputise these already working 'police' as 'community auxiliary police' still under the control of the chiefs, still leaning on traditional means of regulating crime and other major social problems such as the making of home-brew. The policing model in Bougainville today is heavily reliant on these part-time village-based auxiliary police who answer to a village Peace and Good Order (or Mediation) Committee. The New Zealand Government also had the vision to see the virtue of a new post-conflict hybrid that continued to empower the de facto village constables and a new town-based full-time police in Buka, Arawa and Buin. The Western policing model is, however, hegemonically in the hearts even of some of the by and large kindly New Zealand constables[3] sent to assist and among indigenous Bougainvillean police trained in Papua New Guinea sent back to build the new, mostly unarmed Bougainvillean police.

Reintegration of combatants

Three of the 41 seats in the Bougainville House of Representatives were reserved for former combatants. One of the problems of such reintegration through guaranteed power sharing in a democracy is that in Bougainville three seats reserved for combatants also means three seats reserved for males. There were no female combatants in this war. What kind of message would this have been to the women who displayed such magnificent leadership in pushing for peace?

---

3 Australia has also supported police capacity building on and off during the past decade in Bougainville.

So, three seats were also reserved for women. All voters (not just women and ex-combatants) voted for these six seats. The special seats would exist for a maximum of 10–15 years (Wolfers 2006a:9).

Most estimates of the number of Bougainvillean combatants in this war are about 5000 at a maximum. But 15 000 registered as ex-combatants with AusAID's BETA fund to reintegrate ex-combatants through business and training opportunities. In the end, this program funded 2734 applications—mainly from groups of combatants—to a cost of US$2.4 million. There was much fraud. Many men who never fought in the war were funded (UNIFEM 2004:27). In 2006, the PNG Government paid K10 million to Resistance fighters. The final list of claimants totalled 4085.[4] Perhaps this was not such a large amount of money for something that was seen as necessary to push combatants along in seeing the benefits of weapons surrender. Some of the businesses and training that were supported doubtless delivered benefits, but for most this was a hard case to sustain. Trade and hardware stores were funded, provisions were made of stock, feed, agricultural projects, piggeries, bike shops, chicken farms, saws, copra driers, carpentry workshops, boats and motors for fishery, welding supplies, and so on, plus many education projects.

Most of the new recruitment of full-time jobs in the police and as part-time auxiliary police went to ex-combatants. This being so, it is interesting that Bougainvilleans have a reasonably positive attitude towards their police (National Research Institute 2005). An even larger number of ex-combatants got jobs on the AusAID road and bridge rebuilding and repair projects. Only a few of the more senior and more educated combatants got jobs in the Bougainville administration, though many won seats in the House of Representatives beyond those designated for combatants. It is common for younger ex-combatants to feel excluded and 'betrayed' by the comparative success in business and government of their former leaders, while they remain poor (Boege 2008:36).

Refugee rehabilitation

Refugees (mostly in fact internally displaced persons, or IDPs) suffered terribly in the war, after one-third of the population of Bougainville fled their burnt villages. Some suffered in hiding in the mountains, but most were in military-controlled IDP camps called care centres. All of these returned quickly to their villages when peace returned to their region. Unknown but large numbers of the 15 000 to 20 000 mainland New Guineans who fled (Regan 2005b) never

---

4   We are grateful to Edward Wolfers for this information.

returned, largely because they had no BCL-related jobs to return to. The Chinese community never returned to rebuild their businesses because they felt they would not be welcome or free to do so.

Maria Kopiku, in an interview with Patrick Howley (2000:24), recounts insightfully the nature of the damage the care centres did to people and cultures:

> People were crowded together with no privacy; their village groupings were broken up; the network of mutual relationships, associations, interaction and mutual social obligation was suspended. The cultural glue that binds the villages and people together was lost for ten years... Without this glue many people, especially the young lost their sense of respect and shame. Adultery, stealing, domestic violence, lack of respect for elders....became so commonplace...The soldiers who administered the camps were often inconsistent and violent when thwarted. They killed suspect BRA and used their position to steal things and demand women to sleep with. Only now are we seeing the moral damage of the camps in our children who are growing up lacking the values of our society.

There was a considerable investment in trauma counselling in the years immediately after the war. The Marist mission, the Sisters of Nazareth, Caritas and Harvard University played prominent roles in this work, which delivered group or individual counselling to some 20 000 people suffering trauma. While this was a considerable investment, it was not sustained for many years and most people still suffering trauma a decade after the war had no access to professional help. Victims of the war with physical disabilities also did not receive long-term therapy and rehabilitation (Ahai 1999:131).

The Solomon Islands are easily visible from the south of Bougainville, so many people fled there—perhaps 2000 (Reddy 2006:217)—especially the wounded. The PNGDF gave chase into the Solomons at times. This spread aspects of the conflict to that country and worsened the ultimate disintegration of that nation into violence, as we will see in the next Peacebuilding Compared volume on the Solomon Islands.

Conclusion

Refugee and combatant reintegration was much less adequately resourced in Bougainville than in any of the nine Indonesian and Timor-Leste conflicts discussed in the first and fourth volumes of Peacebuilding Compared. In spite of this, kin networks helped most people to rebuild houses and re-establish gardens, and helped them with support from the Church to cope with their trauma. Many years on, the anguish of trauma remains etched on many lives.

The depth, breadth, duration and local ownership of reconciliation are the great comparative strengths of the Bougainville peace. This is even though Bougainvilleans say most of the work of reconciliation remains to be done. This very attention to the glass half-empty reflects the resilience of Bougainvillean reconciliation in comparative perspective. It is hard to think of a case where peacebuilders could learn more from how restorative justice can play a more central role in a peace through studying how indigenous approaches to expanding a peace from islands of civility. That local reconciliation work instructs the peacebuilder to be wary of grand narratives of what a war is about as pointing to the things that need to be reconciled in a particular place. In Bougainville, a particular piece of land or an act of sorcery could be a big issue in what the war was about in that village. Top-down peacemaking does not get at this. Yet these problems can ignite a conflict, just as very local inter-generational conflicts were so vital in starting the conflagration in the first place. We are all familiar with grand narratives as to what World War II was about. For Bougainvilleans, it meant none of these things. They lost many lives in World War II fighting on one side for very different, very local reasons or loyalties. Some chiefs seized on the civil war as an opportunity to settle scars from these World War II conflicts between one village on the side of the Japanese and the other on the side of the allied forces. The historical lesson here is that resilient peace requires attention not just to the top-down settlement of grand geopolitical narratives. It also requires locally meaningful reconciliation that attends to micro-narratives of resentment.

It is to the credit of the Truce and Peace Monitoring Groups that they came to understand the disparate local plurality of conflicts and the trust they could place in local traditions for healing them. Bob Breen nevertheless puts his finger in this chapter on a useful role the internationals played as catalysts. He points out that the hardest part of reconciliation is starting it. And fear of violence is one reason why ordinary folk tremble at making the first move. Truce and Peace Monitoring Group peacekeepers repeatedly made a great contribution in making the move of suggesting a first meeting under their security umbrella. They then had the wisdom to understand that once the conversation was under way, the locals had skills in mediation that they could never attain.

7. The cost of the conflict

The politics of numbers of deaths and the politics of humility

Thus far in Peacebuilding Compared we have encountered conflicts in which the most widely quoted estimates of lives lost from the conflict are considerable underestimates as a result of the state concerned keeping out the international media and non-compliant national journalists or issuing official counts that are underestimates intended to downplay the crisis. These are accepted by lazy journalists as good enough and become the dominant estimates. West Kalimantan (Braithwaite et al. 2010) is an example of such a case. In other cases, international advocates with an interest in exposing such cover-ups of killings counter the cover-ups by producing exaggerated estimates of their own. West Papua in Indonesia is such a case where inflated estimates have become widespread (Braithwaite et al. 2010). Bougainville is in the latter group.

What happened was that the international community woke up one day in the 1990s and realised that what had been occurring in Bougainville for years was not just a 'crisis' or a 'rebellion', but a civil war. In Australia in particular, there was some embarrassment that Australian mining and colonial policy played a big part in the causation of the conflict, that the war was being fought with weapons supplied by Australia and that our media and our leaders had downplayed it. Indeed, the Labor governments of Bob Hawke and Paul Keating had worked with the PNG Government to do so. While the Government of the Solomon Islands allowed the BRA access to their internationally uninfluential media on many occasions to get the terrible story of Bougainville out, on the rare occasions when the BRA leaders got to Australia for peace talks, they were kept away from the media. On at least one occasion, it was an explicit condition of Joseph Kabui's visa that he not speak to the media while in Australia.

The intriguing biography of Alexander Downer in Bougainville

Australia was an ineffective peacemaker in Bougainville during the Hawke and Keating governments because, unlike New Zealand, its policy was to not talk to the BRA. Australia believed the secession of Bougainville would be bad for both

Bougainville and Papua New Guinea as a whole. To be fair, Australia consistently supported a peaceful solution after 1991, resisting waves of pressure from Papua New Guinea to provide greater military support, particularly in equipment for the war. Australia came under pressure from Papua New Guinea for allowing senior BRA member Moses Havini to run an information office in Australia. Havini was married to an Australian citizen. Australian government officials consistently refused to meet with Havini and countered the mostly accurate information he was getting out of Bougainville by satellite phone on atrocities that were occurring in the province with counter propaganda to the effect that Havini was a radical revolutionary who was not a credible source. The Australian media mostly bought this and, during the decade when the war raged, downplayed its horror and significance (Watts 1999). Even the more rigorous and progressive elements of the international media misreported or failed to report the Bougainville war. For example, the *Guardian Weekly* of 7 February 1993 reported the Canberra line of the time that the war was all over, won by the PNGDF: '[T]oday most people, apart from a few Australians, agree that the [Bougainville] rebellion has fizzled out' and only a 'handful of leaderless guerrillas are still active' (Watts 1999:33).

Enter Alexander Downer as the new Foreign Minister in the conservative Howard government. Downer had been meeting with Moses Havini and listening. Like his predecessor, Gareth Evans, Downer was Foreign Minister for more than a decade. He was a less distinguished Foreign Minister than Evans, who had major accomplishments such as the brokering of a UN peacekeeping mission in Cambodia, and even more important contributions as a peacebuilder after leaving politics. But Bougainville was Downer's finest moment, though Downer himself saw East Timor as his finest moment when we interviewed him. When we interviewed Downer's Prime Minister, John Howard, he confirmed that he had more or less left Bougainville policy totally in Downer's hands, except at the height of the Sandline crisis.

In opposition, Downer concluded that the Keating government was handling Bougainville badly. In encounters with Bougainvilleans in opposition and government, he was genuinely touched by their plight and Australia's awful contribution to it. One experience that particularly moved him was accidental. His helicopter had a problem that caused it to land in the Bougainville bush. Where he happened to land, Bougainvillean women were conducting one of the many women's peace marches between BRA and Resistance areas, gathering together in the march women from both sides. He sat down with them for a long talk and the women told him what they wanted him to do to support the peace. Downer did what they asked—and more. Even by his own admission, Downer is hardly a humble man. But he showed humility by allowing New Zealand to lead peacemaking in Bougainville. He allowed New Zealand Foreign Minister,

Don McKinnon, to do much of the front-stage work and take the credit for the international brokering of the peace.[1] He did this because, on the advice of his officials, he believed this was best for the peace—as it was. One of those senior officials said this of the two long-serving Australian foreign ministers of our generation:

> Downer was well suited to Pacific diplomacy with his free-wheeling approach which in Bougainville was pretty effectively responsive to the players. Whereas Gareth could let his frustration get the better of him there. Gareth was better in Cambodia which was better suited to his analytic approach. He was good at working the UN system.

Politicians are normally not very good at allowing other politicians to run away with the credit when they are mobilising most of the dollars for a peacebuilding effort and doing a lot of the hard diplomatic yards behind the scenes. There is no doubt that Howard and Downer played crucial roles in pressuring Papua New Guinea to renege on the contract it had signed with Sandline and using the Australian Air Force to force down the air-freighter transporting Sandline's heavy equipment to Papua New Guinea. Australia leaked much of the inside story on Chan's war plans with Sandline to the international media to put pressure on Chan—at great diplomatic risk to Australia's relationship with Papua New Guinea—though the story was first broken by Mary-Louise O'Callaghan in *The Australian* (Claxton 1998:102).[2] Arguably, there was no greater turning point to peace in Bougainville—and to reviving the fading international norm against mercenaries—than the media getting hold of the planned Sandline invasion of Bougainville. None of this is to downplay the role of New Zealand in the peace. It is simply to locate Downer as a leader of a department that also made important contributions and the New Zealand–Australian partnership as effective because of a certain politics of humility.

Whereas New Zealand's military leader on the ground, Brigadier Mortlock, was advising it to go with the BRA view that it would be prudent for the peacekeepers to be unarmed, Downer had to placate the strongly held view of some generals in the Australian Defence Force that this would be most imprudent. Australian generals were particularly shocked when Mortlock also went along with the BRA view that they should not be required to hand in their weapons as a first priority for the peace process, though again senior Australian Foreign Affairs officer Greg Moriarty supported the Mortlock approach (Regan 2001). Most Australian

---

1 In interviews with senior foreign affairs and military officials involved with Bougainville in New Zealand, and some in Australia, it was said the relationship between McKinnon and Downer was combative. But when we interviewed Downer himself he said he had a good working relationship with McKinnon and Downer respected his great contribution to the peace.

2 Hugh White says he was given the job of leaking the story to Mary-Louise O'Callaghan, but when he called her, she had almost the entire story already—probably from a senior PNG military insider.

generals said they wanted their weapons while the PNGDF were on the ground with their weapons and they also wanted to be able to protect peacekeepers from Francis Ona's forces, should that be necessary. In fact, the deeper reason was that the BRA would negotiate for disposal of weapons to be completed only when a delayed referendum for independence was constitutionally entrenched, and not before then. The top brass in New Zealand also did not warm to Mortlock's approach at first. One New Zealand brigadier, who at first thought Mortlock's support for unarmed peacekeepers among insurgents who were not being disarmed was reckless, told us in an interview that not only did it turn out that this call was right, 'it was profoundly right'.

The risk was not quite as big as it seemed. An Australian Navy vessel with an arsenal was just off the coast of Bougainville during all the years of the peacekeeping operation. While this was never admitted publicly, the BRA leadership was aware of it. If a peacekeeper had been killed in a military attack, the BRA also understood that all the peacekeepers would be withdrawn after armed soldiers secured the withdrawal. This knowledge caused both the BRA and the Resistance to be exceptionally protective of the peacekeepers. For example, in circumstances when an emotionally damaged, drunk ex-combatant was at large with a weapon, locals mounted a 24-hour guard at the peacekeepers' accommodation in a village. It was a unique and complex peace that was being kept here.

When the peace came, Downer derived great personal satisfaction from it. At that point, he put his humility aside and began to tout to Australia and internationally the positive role Australia had played since the election of the Howard government in solving such a major war. In press releases, Downer's advisers settled on the number 20 000 or the more common estimate of 15 000 for the number of deaths caused by the war (Downer 2001:1). The United Nations has also opted for the 15 000 estimate (UN News Centre 2005). Twenty thousand was a big number for such a small population and was widely picked up, reinforcing the appropriate lesson that this was a war that was ignored by the Western world because it was not geopolitically significant in the northern hemisphere. The politics of exaggeration for a good cause is easy to slip into when the only estimates around come from credible sources such as the Australian and New Zealand Departments of Foreign Affairs and statements by the United Nations. But the estimates were baseless.

The elusive count of suffering

The most serious scholar of the conflict, Anthony Regan, has been concerned to offer a corrective to the clear exaggeration in the Downer 20 000 deaths estimate. We judge his statement below to be the most authoritative estimate of the cost of the conflict and more conservative than most estimates in the literature.

> The conflict had terrible impacts. For Bougainville, they included the trauma resulting from perhaps several thousand deaths (at least some hundreds in conflict, many more from extrajudicial killings on all sides, and an unknown number caused or contributed to by the PNG blockade of BRA-controlled areas) and injuries; deep divisions among Bougainvilleans; destruction of most public infrastructure and private-sector productive assets; destruction of the capacity of the local state (the Bougainville provincial government's administrative arm); the large-scale dislocation of life for huge numbers, with up to 60,000 of Bougainville's population of about 160,000 living in refugee camps by 1996.[3] By the time the peace process began, Bougainville had gone from its preconflict status as the wealthiest of PNG's nineteen provinces to among the most impoverished. For PNG, the impacts included hundreds of combat deaths and injuries, massive economic impacts through closure of the mine (which had contributed about 17 percent of government revenues and 36 percent of gross export earnings), and serious impacts on the capacity of the state, including the undermining of the morale of the security forces (in constant crisis from 1989 to 1997). (Regan 2005a:10–11)

We wonder, however, if it is too conservative in correcting the exaggerated accounts that preceded it on the number of combat deaths on the Bougainville side. We code 1000–2000 as the range for the number of conflict deaths. Regan is right that Papua New Guinea suffered 'hundreds of combat deaths'. Many months before the war's end, the PNG Defence Minister said that 200 soldiers and 50 policemen had died on Bougainville (Dorney 1998:320). He had no reason to exaggerate, so we estimate approximately 300 combat deaths on the PNG side. In insurgencies such as the Bougainville war, the objective of the insurgents is

---

3 Sixty thousand is often quoted as the best estimate of the number of IDPs. It is probably too low. It does not include as many as 20 000 (most mainlanders, but also educated Bougainvilleans, Chinese and Europeans), who mostly fled to the mainland (but also to the Solomon Islands—perhaps 500 or as high as 2000 [Zale 1997:23]). It is a count based mainly on estimates of the number in care centres, such as Howley's (2002:65) estimate for 1994 of 42 000 and Amnesty International's (1997:6) for 1997 of 67 000. The biggest cause of the undercount is that many counted in 1994 were no longer in care centres in 1997 and unknown numbers in care centres in 1997 were not there in 1994. That is, both numbers fail to count those in care centres at other times. Finally, there were uncounted thousands of IDPs who fled their burning villages to hide in the bush for a period rather than live in a care centre.

not to inflict a larger number of deaths on the superior army with superior weapons and training that they confront. It is to win by not losing and to inflict sufficient losses for the state to conclude that the military losses it suffers are too high a price. The BRA won the war by not losing in just this sense.

The BRA ended the war in a hurting stalemate in which its forces were more optimistic of victory than the PNGDF.[4] While it had retreated to allow the PNGDF to control most of the territory of Bougainville, the BRA was never defeated in its heartland, and in that heartland and other places as well (from Kangu Beach in the far south to Buka in the far north), it inflicted many significant little defeats on the PNGDF. Even though it was an insurgency in which the insurgents gave a better account of themselves than in most insurgencies, it still recounts as one that fits the pattern of superior state firepower inflicting more deaths on the insurgents than poorly armed insurgents inflict on them (see, for example, Liria 1993). So we assume in the absence of systematic evidence that more than 300 BRA were killed in fighting with the PNGDF. Second, we assume a comparable number of BRA would have been killed in fighting with the Resistance to fighting with the PNGDF. We assume this because the Resistance was on the ground continuously from the time it came into existence, whereas the PNGDF was on the ground only in some places at some times. Moreover, in the place where the PNGDF was on the ground for the longest period, Buka, it stood back and left it to the Buka Liberation Front to do most of the considerable killing of BRA that occurred there. It seems safe to conclude that the number of Bougainvilleans killed in BRA–Resistance fighting on both sides was greater than the number of BRA killed in BRA–PNGDF fighting. So if 300 is a good number for the losses of PNG fighters, if they killed an even greater number of BRA and if an even greater number than that was killed in BRA–Resistance fighting,[5] the number of conflict deaths was way more than 1000. Hence, our coded estimate of 1000–2000. It remains the case, however, that we can only speculate on the number of deaths caused by the blockade and withdrawal of government services (see Regan 1999:557–9). The death toll from being cut off from medicines and professional medical care was certainly high, especially among the elderly who fled their homes.

---

4   BRA military leader Ishmael Toroama did not think there was a hurting stalemate at all: 'We were not tired of fighting. Most of our boys did not agree with us because we were gaining ground.' While he agreed there was a lot of exhaustion among his fighters, he saw the motivation for the peace in terms of the effect the war was having on the children, including the fighting boys themselves being brought up in the way of the gun.
5   Some newspapers have reported 2000 Resistance members killed (Claxton 1999:140). This is most implausible; it would amount to the loss of most of their fighters.

The cost for women

The Leitana Nehan Women's Development Agency told us that they had systematic files on thousands of cases of sexual assault, many by the PNGDF, that were all intentionally destroyed in a PNGDF raid on their premises. These included more than 1000 victims of rape (often with multiple rapists) on Buka Island alone (Saovana-Spriggs 2007:128). We will return to the issue of the cost of the war in terms of a legacy of levels of family violence that did not prevail before the conflict.

Figure 7.1 Helen Hakena holds the UN Millennium Peace Prize for Women awarded to the Leitana Nehan Women's Development Agency, with Peter Reddy in the background

Photo: John Braithwaite

The economic cost

In addition to the loss of royalties, taxes, dividends, thousands of jobs in the mine and thousands of others serving the mine community, all other forms of economic activity declined during the war. Many crops were destroyed or abandoned and fishing became dangerous in many places. Copra production dropped to zero in the early years of the war, then gradually increased to half its prewar level at the end of the war (Lumanni 2005:248). Smallholder cocoa production during the war remained at less than one-third of its prewar peak (Lumanni 2005:255). With considerable development assistance from Australia, the European Union and the UNDP, smallholder cocoa production by 2004–05 had returned to levels similar to the prewar record of 1988–89 (Regan 2007).

Bougainville's micro-finance disaster

One economically debilitating legacy of this conflict is that large parts of Bougainville's banking system have been captured by criminals implementing the philosophy that the best way to rob a bank is to own it. A number of credit unions existed in Bougainville at the beginning of the conflict. All collapsed during the conflict—unable to pay out loans (Shaw and Clarke 2004:12). The institutional collapse associated with civil war allows many kinds of crime to flourish, including financial crime. Micro-finance is important to kick-starting economic development after a war. Conventional Western-style bank finance finds little attraction in lending for investment in post-conflict areas. It is an environment in which credit unions and other models of funding of little people lending to little people are vital to the beginnings of capital investment in business and rebuilding. Bougainville's micro-finance initiatives are, however, weak in comparison with those found in other post-conflict areas.

There have been three legal micro-finance organisations post-conflict—a lot for a population of 200 000. AusAID withdrew funding for one before the scheduled movement from project funding to business funding because of poor management, in spite of early promise (Newsom 2002; Marino 2006:113–14). It was charging 2.5 per cent interest a month on small loans in 2006. Another, funded by the European Union, collapsed as a result of poor management (Shaw and Clarke 2004:12). Two former BRA commanders who ran an ex-combatants' association after they had worked for the other two micro-finance organisations formed another to finance cocoa projects. They had fallen out with other directors of the first two banks. In one case, they described to us the chief executive officer as 'too much of an accountant' who always 'wanted to follow the rules'. This seemed a worrying kind of reason to start a bank.

While micro-finance is vital for creating legitimate opportunities after a war, in postwar environments, it also creates illegitimate opportunities. Prudential supervision of banks is absent on Bougainville's governance landscape. The worst consequence of this has been four pyramid schemes run by Bougainvilleans posing as banks (Shaw and Clarke 2004:12). The largest of these, U-Vistract, created by silver-tongued conman Noah Musingku, has cost a large majority of the families of Bougainville a significant part of their meagre savings, as well as tens of thousands of others in mainland Papua New Guinea and elsewhere in the Pacific (especially Fiji). The modus operandi has allowed some community and political leaders, even the Chief Ombudsman, to make large profits out of U-Vistract and to spread confidence in the 'bank' from the top down. Even President Kabui was a substantial investor in U-Vistract as were other cabinet ministers in Bougainville and Papua New Guinea.

Noah Musingku hooked U-Vistract up with Francis Ona, who was also a large investor. Musingku conned Ona into believing U-Vistract could make the Me'ekamui alternative government in the no-go zone financially viable. More than that, the bank would make Me'ekamui '"the head of the world financial system rather than its tail'". Not long before Ona's death, there was a falling out between Ona and Musingku. Nevertheless, Noah Musingku continued to control part of the Me'ekamui brand and, some of the weapons, and he retained five Fijian soldiers, —two of them former peacekeepers, —to train a small private army in his home village of Tonu. In other words, what we have here is a financial fraudster harnessing a combatant brand -name (Me'ekamui) to defend himself from arrest. U-Vistract has been renamed the Royal International Bank of Meekamui. Its web site claims that it manages US$1 trillion. Noah Musingku has crowned himself His Majesty King David Peii II and as the successor monarch over Ona's kingdom. In a telephone interview with a man who described himself with a chuckle as a spokesman for the King in 2008, John Braithwaite was told, 'President Kabui assured us of amnesty and we assured him we would give him and his men amnesty'!

Thomas Tari (the BRA commander who led the Kangu Beach massacre; Box 4.1) worked with police, who Tari also armed with weapons captured from the PNGDF at Kangu Beach, and led a 'Bougainville Freedom Fighters' attack on Noah Musingku's Tonu 'Royal Palace' in November 2006 in a effort to capture him. After a fire fight that lasted more than an hour, Musingku was wounded, but not captured, and the assault was called off to get a Bougainville Freedom Fighter, who subsequently died, to hospital. In 2010, Musingku remains at large in Tonu, still protected by a dwindling group of armed supporters (Regan 2010).

Figure 7.2 Noah Musingku wearing a crown inscribed 'King' inspects his 'Royal Palace Guards' in Tonu

Photo: *The National*

A mighty cost

While exaggerated accounts of the number killed in the fighting are common, probably considerably more than 1000 were killed directly in the fighting and a larger unknown number died as a result of being cut off from medicines, medical care and their gardens—in many cases as a result of intentional acts of war such as the blockade. Thousands of women and girls were raped. More than one-third of the population lost their homes. A generation of children missed out on an education. All aspects of the export economy collapsed. It is hard to think of a place that has come out of conflict with a more utterly devastated and dysfunctional financial system legacy than Bougainville. The cost of a no-trust banking system in terms of stunted long-term development will be very high, especially if ratings agencies have to assess the financial system of an independent Bougainville and therefore the price it will have to pay for money it borrows.

8. Layers of identity involved in the conflict

The identities invoked in conflicts are consistently coded for the Peacebuilding Compared project. In this chapter, we consider the role of the following layers of identity in this war and this peace: gendered and family identities, big-man and chiefly identities, clan, Bougainville and PNG identities. Of course, there were international identities as well—of the United Nations, Australians, New Zealanders and ni-Vanuatu, who could position themselves as Melanesian *wantoks* of Bougainvilleans because they spoke a similar lingua franca. Both the top-down and bottom-up peacebuilding we have described in the previous chapters can be comprehended as a process of identity work, of pushing forward conciliatory aspects of extant identities and suppressing warlike aspects of those identities. Where many identities are in play in a particular context, there is much scope for local creativity in the identity work of peacebuilding. Such creativity characterised the Bougainville peace.

Gendered and family identities

The most basic layer of meaning for Bougainvilleans is the family identity. For the matrilineal majority—but also in patrilineal areas to a considerable degree[1]—the script 'mother' is unusually wide and profound. It certainly means mother to particular children who issue from a particular mother's womb. Second, it means mother to all the children born in the land over which a set of multigenerational mothers and grandmothers are custodians. Third, it means being mother to all those younger than a particular mother once those children grow into adults. All adults are children of their mothers' land. With modernity, the conception of what is that land of the mothers has widened. So the conception of the women of Bougainville (including those who have not given birth to children) as mothers of the land of Bougainville (Sirivi and Havini 2004; Saovana-Spriggs 2007) is a conception that began to be enlivened only by struggles against colonial conceptions of national boundaries and against the government owning the minerals under the surface of the land that made no sense to Bougainvilleans. The identity mother of the land of Bougainville became stronger in struggles against the conception of nation of fathers of the

---

1 This was clear from our interviews in Buin, Siwai and Nissan. It could be the broad conception of motherhood rooted in custodianship of the land spread as a cultural script (as opposed to one directly connected to custodianship of the land) from the matrilineal to the patrilineal and mixed areas of Bougainville.

new nation of Papua New Guinea (such as Sir Michael Somare from 1975). At the same time, Catholicism, particularly the worship of Mary as the mother of Jesus,[2] has further widened the mother identity to the mother of all humankind. We were told many stories (see also examples in Saovana-Spriggs 2007; Howley 2000) of mothers saying to combatants who were not from their land, including combatants from the PNGDF, 'I am your mother'. Howley (2002:165) provides poetic documentation, for example, of an encounter in which Lucy, President of the Catholic Women's Association in Siwai, calms a shouting PNGDF officer:

> I tell you, when you fight with the young men here, with the BRA and some of you die, maybe you think, we the mothers are happy when we hear about the deaths of your fellow soldiers. I tell you, quite frankly, I am speaking on behalf of the women, when you die or some of you die, we feel very sad too. And if a BRA member dies, I also feel very sad. Because, I do not support the war. I believe in peace. I stand up for peace. And you, even though you are a different coloured skin, you are my son. I am talking to you because I have the heart of a mother. You see, when one of you gets killed, you think, we, the black-skinned people do not care, but that is not true. We care, we, the black-skinned mothers care for you, I am still your mother.

These encounters often effectively regulated the violence of young men or teenagers with guns in the context of that encounter. While soldiers would often argue with Bougainvillean mothers that no, they were not their mother, they had not given birth to them,[3] still there was sufficient of the pan-PNG recognition of this wider cultural script of motherhood for its invocation to at least cause the young man pause, even if he continued with the violence. Just as there were men who promoted peace and men who promoted violence, so there were among the women. While women never in fact fought with guns in Bougainville as far as we can tell, there were many contexts where women supported violence and advocated revenge (see Charlesworth 2008).

---

2   Hermkens (2007) argues that Mary was appealed to by both some in the BRA, who saw the war as a holy war, and peacemakers. Indeed, she argues that Francis Ona did both—daily addressing a statue of Mary during the war to seek her advice and convinced by Mary to seek peace in 1997 on the occasion of the welcoming of the international Pilgrim Virgin Statue of Our Lady of Fatima. The promise to Mary to end the fighting was captured on film (Hermkens 2007:280) and confirmed in our interviews by an Ona aide who was present. Its effect, however, did not make Ona an active supporter of the peace, though he did cease being an active spoiler of the peace in the sense of Ted Wolfers' comment in Footnote 2 in Chapter 6.

3   Helen Ikilai, Siwai schoolteacher, demanding the attention of soldiers:

'Young men, listen to me. We are your Siwai mothers, we are your mothers.' The boys did not accept the claim that these women were their mothers because the women were not their biological mothers. One of the young fighters responded: 'You are not my mother. You did not give birth to me.' Helen replied: 'Regardless of that, myself and all the other women are still your Siwai mothers. You have to believe me' (Saovana-Spriggs 2007:32).

Fourth, the mother script is about custodianship of land, as opposed to simply being people who occupy it today, and all that is spiritually embodied in that land. This includes animals, particularly animals that are totemic of the origin myths of the clan, and the spirits of all one's human ancestors who once physically occupied that land. Catholicism has become increasingly intertwined with a shared spirituality of totemic animals and humans. So in Catholic churches you see animal totems of the clans artistically represented—for example, at the entrance to the church.

Ruth Saovana-Spriggs has provided various quotes from her interviews that capture the potency of women's backstage veto:

> Alright in our case here [Rotokas community], the mothers are the owners [of the land and traditional wealth]. And so, here, men are just like rubberstamps. We, the men cannot say much about land matters. We are just rubberstamps. In my case, if you wish to discuss land with me [with the intention to purchase a piece of land from my lineage], you go and talk to my sisters, not me. They are the ones who say 'yes' or 'no'. But once they say, 'no', then a 'no' is a 'no'. There is no other option. (Interview with Jacob Rerevate, Wakunai, in Saovana-Spriggs 2007:27)

Since land can be seen as everything—as embodying everything—to Bougainvilleans, its custodianship by mothers is a powerful thing for women. Traditionally, it is not a front-stage thing (Kenneth 2005:374), so, at a reconciliation planning meeting about the killing of a number of people that Peter Reddy and John Braithwaite attended on Buka, women on both sides sat on the fringes of the meeting and let their men do most of the speaking for them. 'We let the men do all the talking but if we do not agree with what the men say then women stand up from the back of the meeting and say this is not what the women want' (2006 interview with female leader). They would, however, lean forward and give instructions to their men on what they wanted them to say on their behalf as the landowners. Sirivi and Havini (2004) have documented the most influential interpretation of this articulation of male to female identities:

> The land is sacred and protected by men on behalf of the women. The men as guardians share leadership with women, taking the responsibility in open debate to protect women from potential conflict; however, women have the power to veto decisions, and therefore are involved in the final consultative process. (Sirivi and Havini 2004:149)

One traditional justification for keeping women away from face-to-face political confrontation was that this could sometimes escalate to physical attacks with weapons or death by sorcery. And if mothers who were custodians of the land were killed before their daughters could succeed them, this could cause internal inheritance crises and disputes over distributions of land to different purposes such as digging a new garden (Kenneth 2005:379, 381). Contemporary Bougainvillean feminists see colonialism as having disrupted women's backstage power when *kiaps* designated *luluais* and other male leadership roles (such as 'doctor-boys', who received some first-aid training, and 'bossboys') as the only leadership roles male colonial authority recognised. At the same time, pacification of intertribal warfare dampened the risks associated with taking the front stage in politics. This justifies advocacy in feminist terms of women taking a front-stage role in contemporary politics to counter the way colonialism crushed women's traditional backstage power to instruct and veto. The passive resistance of Rorovana's 'brave matriarchs' in 1969 is often presented as an inspiration for taking that front-stage step:

> Women have put their own safety 'on the line' in Bougainville's stand for their land rights, human rights, justice and freedom and environmental protection. Ever since PNG and Australian police in Loloho beach clubbed the Rorovana mothers to drive them from their Loloho Village property in 1969 there has been an unspoken and unbroken line of resistance. (Havini 1999:40–1)

A theme emerging from some of these quotes is the way war breaks down traditional regulatory relationships of older women and older men—especially of chiefs, male and female—over young men.[4] Peacebuilding in Bougainville has been in part a struggle to reassert something of traditional age-graded identities, which once were highly structured and important, even symbolised on the Bougainville flag through the *upe*—the headgear worn by young men until their transition to adulthood, as pictured on the cover of this book. What are seen as mostly new problems of domestic violence and sexual assault by post-conflict young men are attributed to this breakdown of respect for the guidance of elders (Tonissen 2000). To a degree, community-level peacebuilding has restored this respect for elders.

Big-man and chiefly identities

Older big-men who promoted conflict, such as Francis Ona and Noah Musingku, in a sense started out as young men who put themselves beyond, or partially beyond, the peaceful control of their women. Repeatedly during our fieldwork, we were told that the women of Ona's and Musingku's villages of Guava and Tonu, respectively, were against the war and in favour of peace talks that Ona

---

4   Anthony Regan comments here: 'But I am not convinced on the breakdown argument. It's more that violent conflict destroys or damages balance, and it takes time for a consensus to develop on the need to restore balance rather than fight—and it takes brave leaders, male and female, to move toward that.'

and his hold-outs did not attend. We can only speculate, but it is hard to believe that many women in Guava would not have been opposed to the murder of Ona's uncle, even if there were other women who supported the murder. The younger Ona seemed able to cut himself off from censure by male and female elders. Indeed, once he had demonstrated his willingness to have his way through violence, doubtless elders who wanted peace were afraid to speak up.

Some of the big-men of the war we interviewed were contemptuous of the 'mothers of the land' peacebuilding script. Their line was that it was the BRA leaders who saved Bougainville by leading the war and it was also they, and not the women, who led the peacemaking. Even before the war, it can be argued that the big-man role breaks out of the constraints of matrilineal vetoes and other kinship checks and balances by building constituencies that incorporate many lineages and encompass much wider expanses of land than any kinship group controls. The political practices and identities of modernity allowed a Francis Ona to assert big-manship over all Bougainville. Even Ona, as a chief of Guava, could not totally escape the constraints of the women of Guava—at least in land matters. That was one reason why he did not move on his own to take over the Panguna Landowners' Association, but did it together with the presidency of Perpetua Serero. But as Ona was the pan-Bougainville big-man of the BRA, there were few constraints from BRA women who held sway over him. Hence, the hypothesis that big-manship that is territorially expansive unfetters big-men from the constraints of mothers and of traditional checks and balances more generally.

So we might see big-manship as a Bougainvillean institution (that also exists widely across Melanesia) that structurally enables male subordination of traditional Bougainvillean structures of female empowerment.[5] And we might see warfare in Bougainville society both traditionally and in the 1980s and 1990s as providing an opportunity for new strongmen to break out from female checks and balances and take over. For many very young men, such as Chris Uma, who was a twenty-two year old controlling a large territory during the war, and for Thomas Tari, who was also a twenty-two-year-old commander during the war, the crisis provided a much quicker path to becoming a big-man than, for example, by acquiring the wealth to put on large feasts for a wide circle of people. In Uma's case, maintaining armed roadblocks into a no-go zone that persisted much longer than the war helped sustain that unconstrained power.

---

5   We do not want to be read here as taking a position on the longstanding debates within anthropology about whether matriliny does or does not enhance female power. Yet we do want to argue that big-manship that is territorially expansive cuts big-men off from influence by local sources of female influence, which exist under both matriliny and patriliny, and which can include influence over matters of land, which happen to be particularly important in this conflict. Of course, this would not be such a structurally important matter of gender politics were it the case that there were equal numbers of 'big-women' with geographically expansive influence cut off from local male influence.

The collapse of checks and balances in the West as much as in Melanesia allows big-men to spin fantastic stories about what is responsible for their woes and about prospects for the big-man to deliver the society to some kind of millennial transcendence. Germany was the society with the most sophisticated education system in the world when Hitler spun to its alienated people a fanciful story of how Jews were responsible for the loss of World War I, the Great Depression, inflation, the rise of communism and much more. And he sold the German people a fantastic populist story about how Germany could conquer the Soviet Union, Western Europe, the United States and everyone else to establish a Third Reich that would rule the world. The Japanese militarists managed to sell their people something similar after their early victories in China and Pearl Harbor.

So, we do not need to resort to distinctively Bougainvillean culturalist explanations about cargo-cultism—to visions of a mining policy that will make Bougainville wealthier than Brunei,[6] to visions of the Queen and the President of the United States arriving to pay homage to Bougainville as the future financial capital of the world[7]—as a cargo-cult frame for understanding why Bougainvilleans would follow leaders with ambitions as implausible as Francis Ona's or Noah Musingku's. Ona's vision was not an ambit claim from which he could negotiate a realistic future for international support for greater economic justice, environmental clean-up and political independence for Bougainville. He was a millennial folk hero unhinged from the realities of politics by the excesses a big-man script could allow. The demand for compensation several times larger than the annual national GDP and the lack of interest in compromise—or what Filer (1992:134) somewhat unfairly calls 'the virtual admission of his own insanity'—were about Ona as folk hero. Being above reality checks, it did not matter that there was 'not much method in the madness' (Filer 1992:135). Ona was more prophet who lucked out than politician who made his luck.

Pragmatism did come from people around Ona who did have a politics of greater vulnerability to checks and balances (including from women) and a less murderous politics—men such as Miriung, Kabui, Tanis, Kauona and many others who opted for a revisionist democratic alternative to Ona's kingdom. Yes, there is a history of cargo cults in Bougainville led by big-men who promise fantastically unrealistic things. The most extensively documented one is the Hahalis Welfare Society from the 1960s (Rimoldi and Rimoldi 1992; Oliver 1973). We can opt for cultural explanations of it that scholars more knowledgeable than the present authors might judge to be right. Our purpose is not to challenge the Peter Lawrence (1964) interpretation in *Road Belong Cargo* that cargoism is grounded in distinctively Melanesian epistemologies. It is just to say that we might equally understand cargo cults as consequences of big-men stepping

---

6 President Kabui often made this prediction in his speeches.
7 This is a reference to one of Noah Musingku's predictions for the year 2005.

beyond the checks and balances of traditional Bougainville politics and of the emerging democratic politics and rule of law of PNG/Bougainville society and the important checks and balances in Bougainville society from the regulation of the Church.

The Hahalis Welfare Society put the big-man who led it above the Church, above the state and above the traditional regulatory power of the mothers of the land. Hahalis issued from a credible enough critique of colonial exploitation and domination and an aspiration for cooperative economic development grounded in indigenous values. The society effectively socialised land and other property under the control of the leadership of the society and put girls and young women into a 'baby garden' where they were to be available for sex with sundry men of the society. They were also encouraged to make their sexual services available for sale to outsiders to create wealth for the society. It is hard to imagine a more oppressive deal for women, especially young Catholic women who were told by the ex-communicated leadership of the society that they would have to get used to the idea that this would mean they would end up in Hell (but perhaps God would take pity on them if they kept believing). The hypothesis we advance is that Hahalis was an unrealistic utopian vision of how to transcend colonialism to accumulate cargo and a joyous, wealthy life on Earth because its leaders succeeded in shutting down checks and balances. This included domination of the mothers of the land in their role of asserting the interests of vulnerable girls.

So this is an alternative interpretation to a cultural disposition to believe that there is an easy path to the cargo that white men have traditionally brought and the wealth they have controlled locally. It is one of big-manship as an institution that enables a dismantling of reality checks—from the custodianship of mothers, from the law, from the Church, from education, from investigative journalism and from a robust, contestatory (Pettit 1997) republican politics.

Clan, Bougainville nation, PNG nation

While family, big-man and chiefly identities that transcended female constraints were important in understanding the dynamics of the war, so were other more encompassing identities. Clan was an important one in the sense that certain clan identities could be found right across Bougainville. Leaders of both the war and the peace could invoke clan allegiances across far-flung corners of the province to advance their projects.

Before colonialism, the regional identities—Buin, Siwai, Bana, Nagovis, Nasioi, Tinputz, and so on—were not very important (Kemelfield 1992:156; Oliver 1973; Regan 2005c). They were not units for raising armies or decision-making units in times of peace. They became more important in the plantation economy when workers from different districts were distinguished from one another in this way in order to orient managers and workers to language and cultural differences that had to be navigated to make the workforce click. Naturally, however, in this process of being called a Bana man and revealing important cultural and language differences of Bana from other peoples, men came to think of themselves as Bana men. Similarly, we have already explained how colonial and postcolonial struggles over seemingly unnatural international borders forged the Bougainville identity as increasingly important and ultimately decisive in mobilisation for civil war.

Once the German, British and Australian colonialists had laid down those international boundaries, they of course created an institutional reality on the ground that also sculpted identities. It might be that as a student at the University of Papua New Guinea you joined the Mungkas to assert your Bougainvillean identity, but this resistance was called out because your more encompassing identity there was as a student of the national university of Papua New Guinea. As a member of the Bougainville provincial civil service, you were still a member of the PNG civil service. As a member of a church, you were led by bishops in Port Moresby and listened to sermons from graduates of seminaries and theological colleges on the mainland. And if you became prominent in the church, you shared many moments of communion with mainlanders. In these circumstances, only the most unusual people would not be at all affected by a layer of PNG national identity. Just as Pidgin as a lingua franca and the importance of church identity built bridges between local allegiances that helped constitute pan-Bougainville pacification and a pan-Bougainvillean identity, so Pidgin and the church also contributed to the limited progress towards a PNG national identity.

Conclusion

A complex of identities has therefore been a resource for those who chose to be war-makers and those who chose to be peacemakers, for those who favour integration with Papua New Guinea and for the majority who oppose it at the time of writing. The multiplexity of identities connects the conclusion of this chapter to that of Chapter 6. It is hard to understand how the complex dynamics of the conflict in a particular place demand a particularistic dynamics of reconciliation in that place (as opposed to pursuit of pan-Bougainvillean reconciliation grand narratives). One reason is that the multiplexity of disparate identities—and the history of how they have been mobilised for war and peace—is different in different places.

This is why the Truce and Peace Monitoring Groups—peopled as they were by peacekeepers on six-month rotations—would have been unwise to think of themselves as capable of comprehending the fabric of contextual identities. What they could do was supply a local 'bubble of security' (Shearing 1997) under which parties in conflict could come together in safety and take other risks for the peace. Peacekeepers need to do enough local identity work to understand who the key players are without deluding themselves into believing that they are capable of drawing out the peaceable facets of those identities. They can challenge stereotypes of the other as inherently violent, without presuming they know how to get them to put their non-violent self forward. To their credit, this is pretty much what the mostly humble international peacekeepers did in Bougainville.

9. Interpreting the conflict in summary

This chapter summarises key features of how the Bougainville case will be coded for Peacebuilding Compared. Table 9.1 summarises some key codes that define the section headings in the structure of the chapter.

Table 9.1 Summary of some Bougainville codes; 650 other variables are coded

Structural factors at root of conflict	'Consensus' among analysts that this was a factor or 'contested but credible' as a possible factor?
Colonialism breeds Bougainvillean resentment against specific forms of exploitation by Australia and a Bougainvillean identity resistant to rule from the capital	Contested but credible
General breakdown in law and order. Anomie in a chaotic PNG state	Contested but credible
A qualified 'resource curse' of copper and gold that comes to tempt Francis Ona, Sandline, the PNG state and others to violence.	Consensus
Immigration of ethnic others (especially highlanders) to Bougainville	Consensus
Proximate factors	
The BCL mine displaces communities, destroys the environment, distributes royalties unjustly and opens local divisions between generations and between haves and have-nots	Consensus
Human rights abuses, arson and payback from PNG security forces	Consensus
Decisions not to renegotiate the BCL agreement in 1981 and 1988 in accord with 1974 agreement	Contested but credible
Myriad local proximate factors such as land disputes, sorcery, grabs for local political ascendency	Consensus
Key triggering incidents	
Demolition of electricity pylons	Consensus
Rape/murder of nurse	Consensus

Key Warmaking Actors	
PNG security forces	Consensus
Bougainville Revolutionary Army (especially Francis Ona)	Consensus
'Skin BRA' and raskols (semi-organized criminal groups)	Consensus
Resistance	Consensus
Sandline (almost!)	Consensus
Ted Diro and PNG political hawks	Consensus
Key Peacemaking Actors	
Women leaders like Sister Lorraine Garasu	Consensus
BRA and Resistance leaders and non-aligned moderates like John Momis	Consensus
PNG leaders – Peter Barter, Moi Avei, Bill Skate, and others	Consensus
The crowd on the streets of Port Moresby backed by the PNGDF demanding termination of the Sandline contract	Consensus
Church and other local peace NGOs such as the Peace Foundation Melanesia and the Leitana Nehan Women's Development Agency	Consensus
Theodore Miriung and other peace zone leaders	Contested but credible
International NGOs (eg, Red Cross and Solomon Islands Christian Association)	Contested but credible
Truce and Peace Monitoring Groups	Consensus
New Zealand diplomats	Consensus
The United Nations supported by regional leaders like Billy Hilly, Alexander Downer and their diplomats	Consensus
Advisors to peace process participants (eg Anthony Regan)	Consensus
Chiefs and other leaders of traditional reconciliations	Consensus
Peacebuilding strengths	
Local dialogue and thousands of reconciliations building ever-wider zones of reconciliation. Leadership for peace of women and men in networked civil society	Consensus
International peacekeepers increasing confidence to expand zones of peace and tackle new reconciliations	Consensus
Local control of the top-down peace process	Consensus

Trust and commitment built by agreement to link sequenced moves to peace tit-for tat. Innovative credible commitment architecture	Contested but credible
Reduction of rape, violence, carrying of guns and crime post-conflict except in parts of the south (enabled by reassertion of traditional village authority over young men). Domestic violence still a big problem, however.	Consensus
Reintegration of combatants into the government elite, the police, village economies, cacao production and some paid employment (though much of it not sustainable)	Contested but credible
Rapid resettlement of Bougainvillean refugees in their villages and closure of refugee camps	Consensus
Peacebuilding weaknesses	
Peacekeepers leave with Me'ekamui not integrated into the peace, a large No Go Zone secured by armed roadblocks and many weapons not destroyed	Contested but credible
No Bougainville consensus achieved on how to deal with the likely re-opening of the mine	Consensus
Post-conflict international diplomacy fails to put PNG under pressure to accept that it must either persuade the people of Bougainville to vote for integration or to accept their decision for independence	Consensus
Reconciliation of Bougainville with PNG security forces and leaders, with mainland and Chinese refugees neglected	Contested but credible
Building a Bougainville state proceeds weakly. Aid floods in early when absorption capacity is low, then declines when it is most needed.	Contested but credible
Programs for youth neglected; trauma counselling energetic at first, but not sustained	Consensus
Failure to mobilise most of the highly educated Bougainville diaspora to return home to support the redevelopment of Bougainville	Consensus
Financial regulation is a disaster area	Consensus

Structural factors at root of conflict	'Consensus' among analysts that this was a factor or 'contested but credible' as a possible factor?
Colonialism breeds Bougainvillean resentment against specific forms of exploitation by Australia and a Bougainvillean identity resistant to rule from the capital	Contested but credible
General breakdown of law and order. Anomie in a chaotic PNG state	Contested but credible
A qualified 'resource curse' of copper and gold that comes to tempt Francis Ona, Sandline, the PNG state and others to violence	Consensus
Immigration of ethnic others (especially Highlanders) to Bougainville	Consensus
Proximate factors	
The BCL mine displaces communities, destroys the environment, distributes royalties unjustly and opens local divisions between generations and between haves and have-nots	Consensus
Human rights abuses, arson and payback from PNG security forces	Consensus
Decisions not to renegotiate the BCL agreement in 1981 and 1988 in accordance with 1974 agreement	Contested but credible
Myriad local proximate factors such as land disputes, sorcery, grabs for local political ascendency	Consensus
Key triggering incidents	
Demolition of electricity pylons	Consensus
Rape/murder of nurse	Consensus
Key war-making actors	
PNG security forces	Consensus
Bougainville Revolutionary Army (especially Francis Ona)	Consensus
'Skin BRA' and raskols (semi-organised criminal groups)	Consensus
Resistance	Consensus
Sandline (almost!)	Consensus
Ted Diro and PNG political hawks	Consensus
Key peacemaking actors	
Women leaders such as Sister Lorraine Garasu	Consensus
BRA and Resistance leaders and non-aligned moderates such as John Momis	Consensus
PNG leaders Peter Barter, Moi Avei, Bill Skate, and others	Consensus

The crowd on the streets of Port Moresby backed by the PNGDF demanding termination of the Sandline contract	Consensus
Church and other local peace NGOs such as the Peace Foundation Melanesia and the Leitana Nehan Women's Development Agency	Consensus
Theodore Miriung and other peace-zone leaders	Contested but credible
International NGOs (for example, the Red Cross and Solomon Islands Christian Association)	Contested but credible
Truce and Peace Monitoring Groups	Consensus
New Zealand diplomats	Consensus
The United Nations supported by regional leaders such as Francis Billy Hilly, Alexander Downer and their diplomats	Consensus
Advisors to peace process participants (for example, Anthony Regan)	Consensus
Chiefs and other leaders of traditional reconciliations	Consensus
Peacebuilding strengths	
Local dialogue and thousands of reconciliations building ever-wider zones of reconciliation. Leadership for peace of women and men in networked civil society	Consensus
International peacekeepers increasing confidence to expand zones of peace and tackle new reconciliations	Consensus
Local control of the top-down peace process	Consensus
Trust and commitment built by agreement to link sequenced moves to peace tit for tat. Innovative credible commitment architecture	Contested but credible
Reduction of rape, violence, carrying of guns and crime post-conflict except in parts of the south (enabled by reassertion of traditional village authority over young men). Domestic violence, however, still a big problem	Consensus
Reintegration of combatants into the government elite, the police, village economies, cacao production and some paid employment (though much of it not sustainable)	Contested but credible
Rapid resettlement of Bougainvillean refugees in their villages and closure of refugee camps	Consensus

Peacebuilding weaknesses	
Peacekeepers leave with Me'ekamui not integrated into the peace, a large no-go zone secured by armed roadblocks and many weapons not destroyed	Contested but credible*
No Bougainville consensus achieved on how to deal with the likely reopening of the mine	Consensus
Post-conflict international diplomacy fails to put Papua New Guinea under pressure to accept that it must either persuade the people of Bougainville to vote for integration or accept their decision for independence	Consensus
Reconciliation of Bougainville with PNG security forces and leaders, with mainland and Chinese refugees neglected	Contested but credible
Building a Bougainville state proceeds weakly. Aid floods in early when absorption capacity is low, then declines when it is most needed	Contested but credible
Programs for youth neglected; trauma counselling energetic at first, but not sustained	Consensus
Failure to mobilise most of the highly educated Bougainville diaspora to return home to support the redevelopment of Bougainville	Consensus
Financial regulation is a disaster area	Consensus

* It is not contested that these are problems, but more than one commentator remarked '[m]ight it not be regarded as a particular strength of the Bougainville peace process that it has proceeded without Me'ekamui's participation, while inviting them to join in—thereby making it difficult for Me'ekamui to prevent the peace process from moving ahead'.

What structural factors were at the root of this conflict?

Ron May (1990:57) suggested that the civil war was 'to some extent a ripple effect from the more general breakdown of law and order and challenge to the authority of the state which has characterised the recent political history of so many other parts of Papua New Guinea' (see also Filer 1992:118). This has some similarity to the analysis of the first volume of Peacebuilding Compared on Indonesian conflicts. After the fall of President Suharto, there was a ripple effect in a breakdown of law and order that spread from one to another place in Indonesia. And this was about a condition of anomie during that period of Indonesian history, when the rules of the political game were up for grabs and a condition of normlessness prevailed. The difference between Indonesia and Papua New Guinea was that Indonesia experienced an anomic transition from a remarkably unified autocratic national society (given its size, archipelagic spread and ethnic diversity) to a remarkably unified democratic national society after six years of social and political disintegration and unusual levels of violence. Papua New Guinea, in contrast, started life in 1975 as an impressively democratic developing country that seemed in the 1960s and 1970s to be developing towards unified nationhood and coherent national institutions of law, public administration, education and democratic governance. Papua New Guinea has averted a collapse of its democracy into the kind of autocracy that Indonesia experienced under Sukarno and Suharto. But since 1980 it has been continuously a much more violent, socially disintegrative, anomic national society than it was in the decades after pacification.

Colonialism did not deal with Bougainville sensitively. 'Bukas' were favoured for 'blackbirding'—for what was in many cases effective plantation slavery in other parts of Papua New Guinea and in North Queensland. We met one prominent Me'ekamui Defence Force commander who imagined that his father had been blackbirded, though given his age, it would not have been likely that even his grandfather could have been blackbirded. The point is, however, that blackbirding is part of a fabric of colonial resentment that does have a real and disturbing historical basis. Another strand of the fabric of resentment against colonialism was the arbitrary drawing of the international boundary between Papua New Guinea and the Solomon Islands. As Bougainvilleans stand on Kangu Beach and look across to the nearby Solomon Islands populated by folk racially identical to them, whose ancestors migrated to places such as Kangu Beach and Rorovana to establish the communities there, with whom they have traded for centuries, they wonder why did the '*waitman*' put us in the same country with the 'redskins'?

World War II caused huge suffering and loss of life among Bougainvilleans. Both sides committed terrible atrocities against Bougainvilleans who helped the other side. Some of the World War II resentments of one community being turned against another became scores to be settled in the civil war after 1988. Resentment against both sides of the imperial struggle was evident in the village in Selau where John Braithwaite lived in 1969. The men had been forced to work building the Buka airstrip by the Japanese. Each time it neared completion, American bombers would turn it into a string of craters. The Japanese tried to foil this by forcing the men to continue to work instead of fleeing the strip when the bombers came in. The young American commander of the bombers came around twice after aborted bombing runs during which the Bougainvilleans had not run from the strip as in the past. On the third pass, he bombed them as the women and children looked on in horror. When a patrol boat supplied by

Australia to Papua New Guinea 46 years later fired on the village, this was again seen as a case of the *waitman*'s horrific war machines hailing destruction on the innocents of the village.

Colonialism was seen as bringing 'redskins' not only at the helm of patrol boats, but for many decades before that as workers on Australian plantations in Bougainville. Cultural clashes with mainland plantation workers were modest before the mine brought expanded numbers of mainland workers to Bougainville. But they had happened enough to connect up to a narrative of a long history of invasion and colonial exploitation. The Chinese, who Bougainvilleans viewed as commercially exploitative, had also initially been brought to work European plantations. The forging of a pan-Bougainvillean identity conceived in opposition to PNG institutions—while it had some stirrings in these resentments—did not really take off until the mine gave it one big focus. Even today, much more local identities remain more important than a Bougainvillean identity. But during the past four decades the Bougainvillean identity has become profound—and much more real than a PNG identity. This is of course now a social structural source of separatism.

We have seen that immigration of mainlanders threatened the way of life of locals and caused tensions through squatting on land and most importantly crime problems at a level that Bougainvilleans had never experienced. Not only did Bougainvilleans feel a threat to their sense of self-determination on their own land, around the mine, they felt downright unsafe. Because of this history, a new wave of migration at a much lower level is therefore a potential future threat to the peace that must be watched closely. This is the gradual inundation of Carteret Island offshore, which is requiring resettlement of 2500 Carteret Islanders on the Bougainville mainland.

What have been the proximate factors in the conflict?

Opening the Panguna mine was the crucial proximate factor in this conflict. This does not necessarily mean the Bougainville case supports the resource-curse hypothesis as formulated by Collier (2007) and others (see Regan 2003). The mine was not looted to support the start-up costs of the insurgency. It also did not extend the war by providing lootable resources for the BRA. The resource curse might have escalated the war through the agency of Sandline, who proposed a share of the post-conflict loot as payment for their services. Paradoxically, Sandline's resource diplomacy played out to shorten the war. Some of Francis Ona's inner circle started the war with the ambition of closing the mine forever. Ona himself started the conflict intent on getting a better deal for landowners and for Bougainville from the mine. To that extent, there was a resource curse. Moreover, once the war was under way, many Bougainville leaders—Sam Kauona and Joseph Kabui included—were pushing on for independence rather than a peace deal within Papua New Guinea because they believed that even though Bougainville was tiny, they could make it fiscally viable by reopening the mine. To that extent, a resource curse was an incentive to spurn an early peace on Papua New Guinea's terms.

Finally, and most fundamentally, we have seen that a resource curse did drive grievances among locals over equitable compensation, class conflict over job and educational opportunities, displacement of villages, environmental destruction, invasion by 'redskins' who were perceived as violent—and all this motivated violent resistance (Ross 2004; Regan 2003). Like the Indonesian cases of Peacebuilding Compared, the Bougainville case illustrates that there is no structural inevitability of a resource curse. Today, this is clearer than ever. Divisions within the Bougainville and PNG polities over if and how to reopen the mine could trigger new conflict. On the other hand, strong, listening leadership and just handling of the issue could deliver Bougainville consensus over a mine reopening that would accelerate educational and employment opportunities, fund health services and other drivers of development and begin to clean up some of the environmental destruction from past mining. If that could be accomplished, it would consolidate peace.

The slapdash micro-management of land-title issues from the 1960s by the PNG Administration, the Land Titles Commission and BCL opened up great internal divisions among landowners about who was responsible for the disaster the mine inflicted on their lives and who would collect the windfall from the cash it rained. This war started as a conflict among landowners where a frustrated, aggrieved and in some cases greedy younger group resorted to violence to push aside their elders and make unrealistic demands on the company. By unrealistic, we mean that the company would rather close than pay what the New Panguna Landowners' Association asked, which is what it did. It was also unrealistic in the sense that the closure of the mine could be something the rest of Papua New Guinea would just accept. The leaders of Papua New Guinea at the time had no political choice but to use all means possible to get the mine reopened. Even today, after all that has happened, many senior Panguna landowners do not understand the economic realities of what a mine can and cannot deliver. The root cause of this situation is the poor quality of dialogue held with the landowners in the two decades before the war broke out.

Because the mine brought such a huge amount of public money for the development of Papua New Guinea, it was never a project any government would say no to, whatever the local landowners thought. Given the sheer size of the mine, the hugeness of the physical impact on land that was many people's lives, the unmanageability of the environmental impact downstream given this magnitude, the geography and the state of the art of environmental management technology in the 1960s and 1970s, it was always going to be the case that many landowners would be devastated. By the late 1980s, pipeline technology for tailings disposal had improved and when the war closed the mine a pipeline project was 70 per cent complete (Vernon 2005:269). The landowners would be shattered by what happened to their land once those powerful hoses started blowing away the soil from under their trees and villages and those trees and houses began to topple into the huge hole where their lives were once lived. Even very sophisticated Bougainvilleans, like their member in the National Parliament, Sir Paul Lapun, did not understand the hugeness of the hole and the impact that was being agreed to in advance of the land being blown away for that hole. A dialogue with locals was needed that comprehended the full sadness of what was bound to happen to their land.

What was not inevitable was that there would be deep, murderous, internal division in how to respond to it. What was not inevitable was the injustice (and slapdash arbitrariness) in how the financial compensation for the tragedy of the land was distributed. What was not inevitable was that there would be a civil war. An honest, respectful dialogue starting in the 1960s about the scale of the environmental tragedy of the blowing away of the land and about why that was politically inevitable were what was needed to avoid the war. Compensation for local landowners was then needed that was more proportionate to the devastation their lives were about to suffer. Then careful collaborative investigation was needed about the nature of the ownership of the land by matrilineal clan lineages. Instead, what happened was that individual men or women who stepped forward and said they were landowners were duly recorded as individual title-holders as long as some community members who were at a particular meeting did not disagree—if indeed they understood what was going on given the language challenges of the communication (Regan 2007). In a number of cases, according to Regan (2007), senior men listed as title-holders favoured particular nieces and their families over others, opening up divisions within lineages.

Yes, poor environmental management was also a proximate factor in the conflict, in that fewer people might have had their fields and fisheries devastated downstream with better environmental management. The environmental devastation could have been much less, and if it had been, some people would have been less angry, but there still would have been widespread anger.

The fact that this was an Australian mine connected resentment over Australian colonialism to this string of acts of micro-mismanagement in the 1960s and early 1970s. The failure to have the kind of just and locally attuned dialogue that might have reconciled people to the mine was a factor that fuelled this conflict.

But there were later missed opportunities to undo some of this damage in a way that might have saved the peace. We have seen that John Momis believes that if the Chan government had allowed the agreed renegotiation of the mine agreement that fell due in 1981 to proceed, the war could have been prevented. After all, the very reason a seven-year renegotiation cycle was provided for was to monitor and head off any escalation of conflict. Even the next seven-year renegotiation due in 1988 might not have been too late.

A less retributive form of policing than the human rights abuses and burning of villages indulged in by the riot police and then the military might also have averted escalation to civil war. The PNG security forces should have been capable of seeing the risk of resistance breaking out all over the powder keg that was Bougainville in 1988–89. And they should have seen that if this happened they lacked the logistics and the boots on the ground to put this down. More fundamentally, this was a problem of their policing model being that of a militia as opposed to a community policing model that solved problems by listening to communities and to the solutions they proposed.

We have seen that the proximate cause of conflict in a particular area could have been *raskol*ism by a particular group, sorcery by a particular individual, levelling directed at new educated elites, using the war as a pretext to solve an old land dispute or just to steal cars and other property from a village more wealthy than one's own.

It is often difficult to say whether armed conflict is more about greed than grievance (Collier 2007). Many BRA informants alleged the Resistance fought for PNG money. These do not seem plausible allegations in terms of most Resistance fighters, whose support from Papua New Guinea was barely sufficient to maintain them as a credible fighting force, let alone support them to live well. There were more credible allegations that one senior Resistance military commander was on the take. PNGDF sources who make these allegations dismiss the analysis that the Resistance in general was motivated by greed.

A number of people we interviewed alleged that many of the Me'ekamui hold-outs were holding out as a money-making strategy. It was alleged one Me'ekamui commander had been paid K50 000 to allow the 2007 election to proceed peacefully in his area. Roadblocks were used to collect payments to pass from certain kinds of people (generally not poor locals). Payment was also solicited and paid for what was hoped would be the permanent dismantling of roadblocks. Some Me'ekamui leaders were seeking to commercialise reconciliations, indicating that they would participate in reconciliation ceremonies only if they were paid unusually large amounts of cash. As with our discussion of the resource-curse hypothesis, some greed is parasitic on a considerable number of grievances that were the primary proximate factors in this conflict.

What were the key triggering incidents?

The demolition of the electricity pylons on the road to the mine in 1988 followed by shooting at the workers who arrived to repair it triggered escalation. It put BCL onto an exit footing and therefore put the PNG security forces on emergency footing.

One senior and credible informant in the Bougainville Government had the view that the war would not have occurred if the nurse had not been raped and murdered in 1988, though he was the only one we heard express a view as decisive as this.

BRA military commander Sam Kauona (2001:85) expressed it this way:

> One of the causes of the crisis was outsiders—non-Bougainvilleans from other parts of Papua New Guinea—raping and terrorising our women. Many people from my area in Central Bougainville joined the struggle following the brutal murder of one of our women at the back of Aropa Plantation by plantation workers. People said, 'That is enough: we have to join now—we have to support our women.'

At the very least, this rape/murder triggered an important phase in the escalation of the conflict.

Who were the key war-making and peacebuilding actors?

Neither side planned or wanted a war with the other. Francis Ona was the key war-maker on the Bougainville side. When violence broke out against 'redskins' after the murder of the nurse, Ona had no plan, but 'rode the emotion' by calling the young men out (Ona aide interview). He became a magnet for people with various grievances, particularly about the sharing of benefits from the mine and its environmental impact, and others far from the mine who wanted independence. Ona embraced them all as they all contributed to building a wave of resistance to the state on the crest of which Ona was able to ride as a uniquely big big-man in the history of Bougainville. Ona was a man with a large ego who rode a wave of anti-PNG, anti-BCL, anti-Australian emotion to become very famous—indeed revered—for the boldness of his resistance.

The other key war-making actors are clear enough: Ted Diro and his hawkish following in Port Moresby, the PNG security forces, the Resistance and skin BRA and other *raskol* elements causing conflict by pretending to be BRA or the Resistance. And of course Sandline were paid to be mercenaries, but did not manage to get a shot off to earn their millions. We often make the mistake in writing about this war, including in this book, of reifying 'the Resistance' as an army backed by Papua New Guinea fighting the BRA. The reality of 'the Resistance' for many villages was a home guard that eschewed offensive operations against the BRA; their 'Resistance' was an expedient to defend themselves after strict neutrality proved difficult to sustain when confronted with marauding 'BRAskols' and assassinations of peace leaders. Much the same was true of many BRA elements.

It is hard to overestimate what a difficult thing it must have been for Sam Kauona, Joseph Kabui, Ishmael Toroama, James Tanis and so many less senior BRA figures to take their different fork in the road from Francis Ona. These leaders still spoke of Ona with respect, even reverence, in 2006 and 2007. Ishmael Toroama does not figure often in our text, but he mattered greatly. He was a leader men followed. He was an extraordinarily effective insurgency commander who decimated PNGDF patrols again and again. He had personal courage that few human beings have. He captured the very first PNGDF automatic weapons by attacking two armed soldiers with a crossbow; he killed the first with an arrow at close quarters, then shot the second with the gun of the first. Without Toroama's backing, Kabui could never have become President of the ABG. We asked his successor, James Tanis, what was the contribution to the peace he was most proud of. His answer was persuading Ona not to kill John Momis when Ona captured him in 1997 and ordered Tanis to kill him. Tanis believed Momis was a respected leader who was vital for persuading moderates to join the BRA in what ultimately became a national unity grand coalition government (dominated by former BRA) that held together the peace. Momis and Ona reconciled and went on the radio together urging all Bougainvilleans to reconcile as they had done (Tanis 2002b). Ironically, three years after this interview with James Tanis, he lost a tough presidential election campaign against John Momis just as this book went to press.

Most PNG Ministers for Bougainville Affairs made major contributions to the peace: Peter Barter, Moi Avei, Sam Akoitai, Michael Somare and Mekere Morauta (though the important contributions of the last were as prime minister). There were also big contributions by other PNG Prime Ministers, especially Bill Skate, who backed Barter's plan and Theodore Miriung's legacy. Skate, according to one senior PNG official was Papua New Guinea's most corrupt prime minister, while Sir Julius Chan was its most hard-working one. Yet 'Skate was the first prime minister to go into the bush in Bougainville. He was respected in Bougainville.[1] He was seen as sincere in how he listened to people. He was a good listener. Sir

---

1 Not universally, however, as a result of his formidable alcohol intake and some other excesses to which some took offence.

Julius Chan was into monologue.' The crowd on the streets of Port Moresby made history in 1997 protesting the Sandline contract in a way that utterly destabilised Prime Minister Chan, opening the path for the new Prime Minister Skate to find common cause with the BRA and the PNGDF.

PNG public servants such as Chief Secretary, Robert Igara, and Director of Bougainville Affairs, Bill Dihm, made major backroom contributions. Many outstanding New Zealand diplomats also worked especially effectively in conspiring with Barter in Port Moresby for peace, with the backing of their Foreign Minister, Don McKinnon. Many equally anonymous Australian diplomats were effective in quietly supporting the New Zealanders. Senior Australian military officers in Bougainville—unlike some in Canberra— were also impressive in the way they followed in the peacekeeping pattern set by the passionate and culturally deferential leadership of New Zealand TMG Commander Brigadier Roger Mortlock. Then there were the leaders of humanitarian organisations such as the Red Cross (whose family and village packs helped survival, who were hated by the PNGDF for insisting on rights under international humanitarian law in the care centres and distrusted by the BRA because they believed the Red Cross worked with Australian spies) and UNICEF (whose school packs helped get education moving again, including in the no-go zone). The UNDP and the United Nations more broadly were also very important in getting behind peace and development, including through support for reconciliation logistics. Noel Sinclair and his successors played vital political roles as heads of UNOMB. Anthony Regan is one advisor to the parties whose mighty behind-the-scenes contributions to the peace on the Bougainville side are widely recognised. But there were other very important advisors such as Ted Wolfers on the PNG side, Ian Prentice, Leo White and Mark Plunkett and many other fine civil servants.

All of these individuals were major contributors to the top-down peace. But we have seen that the big thing about Bougainville was that the top-down accomplishment was built on the foundations of a bottom-up accomplishment. From 1990, female and male elders and church leaders were going out into conflict areas persuading their young men to down weapons and help create their village as an island of civility. In one of Peter Reddy's 2004 interviews, a former guerrilla platoon leader explained how his sister urged him to participate in the Arawa Peace Conference of 1994: 'In our culture, you are supposed to listen to your sister. If she gives you advice, you are supposed to take it' (Reddy 2006:226). Because such large swathes of the people had deserted their war under such bottom-up influences, the BRA leaders had to take the top-down peace seriously.

Many were assassinated in promoting reconciliation—not just high-profile peacemakers such as Theodore Miriung and John Bika. Less prominent individuals who were killed included three members of the Peace Foundation Melanesia doing their work to promote restorative justice as a path to peace. Peacemakers from the church were also assassinated. A peace leader such as Sister Lorraine Garasu took countless risks with her life and continues to do so as she works to expand the peace into the no-go zones. She struggles for funding in that work, saying she is too tired to keep filling out grant applications. That should be one of the lessons of Bougainville. Because it is a peace erected so fundamentally on the reconciliatory work of Sister Lorraines, a Sister Lorraine might have been given a living allowance and a car so that she could be Sister Lorraine. Sister Lorraine is exhausted so much of the time because travel in Bougainville is exhausting without a vehicle. No grant applications, no accountability, no evaluation reports—just trust and a ceremony in which the car is handed over and she makes public commitments on the peace work she will use the car to advance. An international discretionary fund freed from accountability constraints that a foreign ambassador in Papua New Guinea could go to and say simply, 'Please buy Sister Lorraine a car and give her a living allowance', would add greatly to capacity for many outstanding individuals to lead peace from the bottom up. Individual peacekeepers—privates or non-commissioned officers from Vanuatu, for example—count alongside the countless Bougainvilleans who have contributed locally to the bottom-up peace.

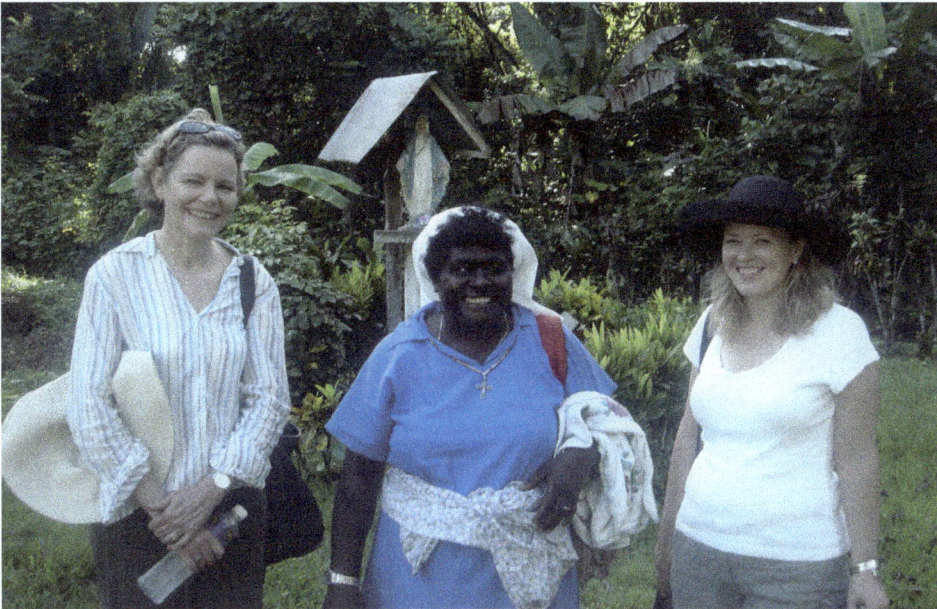

Figure 9.1 Hilary Charlesworth, Sister Lorraine Garasu and Leah Dunn, Chabai 2007

Photo: John Braithwaite

President Kabui saw the Solomon Islands Council of Churches as an important contributor to the peace through both its mediation in the Solomon Islands and its lobbying of the Pacific Council of Churches, then the World Council of Churches to internationalise the peace effort.

It seems invidious to list the particular names we have in the preceding paragraphs—invidious because there are so many other names that are equally worthy. Yet it is important to illustrate the diversity of kinds of individual leadership in a bottom-up–top-down peace such as Bougainville's. The same invidiousness arises in nominating Bougainvilleans for deeply deserved peace prizes—something we have done in the cause of getting the story out to the northern hemisphere of why they should take notice of the Bougainville accomplishment. One cynical interviewee, who was a major contributor to the peace, said 'peace prizes are a menace to peace'. By this he meant that by making celebrities of one or two individuals when there are in fact thousands who deserve that praise, two bad things happen. One is that some individuals can become self-promoters rather than the needed self-effacing collaborators for peace who praise others but not themselves. The second is that peace activists who think that those singled out for prizes are less deserving than others can disparage their work, even to the point where securing funding becomes harder for them as a result—something that has happened in Bougainville. We wonder if a different kind of peace prize might better serve the diffused reality of leadership of the most effective peace processes that is so evident in this case. This would be to award the prize to all the individuals who contributed to the peace. This could be a peace prize awarded to 'The people of Bougainville and its friends who worked for the Bougainville peace'. Instead of investing in airfares for winners, prize banquets for suits, cash prizes and lumps of silver, a cash contribution to funding a 'Bougainville Peace Prize Museum' as a tourist attraction might be more constructive, with that start-up funding matched by admission charges to tourists, donations from peacekeepers and other internationals who served the peace, and from local businesses (and the state), which might see economic benefits from such a tourist attraction. The philosophy of a Peace Prize Museum could be to represent the very diversity of the types of cooperative contributions to the peace that is one lesson the world should learn from a peace such as Bougainville's.

The Australian Government fits the common pattern of an actor that contributed to the war and to the peace. Its colonial laws and policies allowed disastrous terms for the construction of the mine. It supplied helicopters to the PNGDF on condition that they not be used as gun-ships in Bougainville, when leaders knew they would be so used. And it supplied much more that destroyed lives. It was only after 1993 that Australia forcefully applied pressure on Papua New Guinea to opt for a peaceful solution, though from that time it did so persistently and constructively. Anthony Regan has an intriguing way of viewing the paradox of the failure of the regional power to take the lead until after the peace was largely sealed:

> In retrospect, it seems clear that Australia's diffidence about its role contributed to the positive outcomes of the whole process. Had Australia sought to play the more expansive and agenda-setting role (directed particularly at accelerating the pace of the process) [in particular, Australia wanted to exit the Peace Monitoring Group much earlier] that some key Australian figures would have preferred, it is likely that there would have been considerable resistance to the intervention. There would have been far less room for the unfolding local dynamics that permitted the resolution of tensions and reconciliation of differences. (Regan 2005a:24)

Peacebuilding strengths and weaknesses

Local ownership

Perhaps the greatest strength of peacebuilding in Bougainville has been its local ownership. New Zealand leadership of the international intervention did not impose solutions; it provided a secure environment in which factions had to reach their own accommodations (Regan 2010). The intervention facilitated and supported locals who set the agendas. AusAID funded independent advisors to all parties involved in negotiation of the Bougainville Peace Agreement. But it did this only because of requests for support from specific parties for specific advisors they trusted (Regan 2010). Distinctive strengths we have discussed— such as the bottom-up restorative justice resilience of traditional reconciliation and the linked sequencing of credible commitments—did not arise from any grand plan of outside state builders. They evolved dynamically out of conversations among the main factions—each step a response to what happened at the last step to peace. That is not to say it was all incoherent incrementalism. Far from it. Some of the incremental steps were agreements to craft encompassing constitutional designs—indeed designs that linked coherent constitutional re-engineering to wider aspects of the political settlement. That is to say that it was an accomplishment of a fairly deliberatively democratic process, not the imposition of any mastermind of either a Washington neo-liberal consensus or a socialist plan. Outsiders contributed greatly when they were asked, and mostly when they were given a brief grounded in a deliberated consensus of locals.

In these respects, Bougainville makes an interesting contrast with Timor-Leste. Some senior Australian police, for example, take a lesson to be learned from

Timor-Leste as that 'too many cooks spoiled the broth'. International advisers from one nation's police would come in to tell the Timor-Leste police in a particular district to do X. Then another nation's police would be rotated in and would say do not do X, do Y. Reform went in circles, without coherence. So the lesson learned for application in the Solomon Islands was that one nation (Australia!) should impose the coherence on police reform. In contrast, Bougainvilleans took the lesson from their peace to be reliance on a deliberated consensus of locals to secure coherence. Be wary of outsiders (especially Australia!) who disrupt coherence by dominating local voices and rushing to meet timetables before local consensus is sorted. Make sure you draw on the resources of many international fonts of advice and technical assistance and support, because if one of them (especially Australia!) offends key factions in respect of some arena of governance, it is possible to turn to another and ask them to specialise their assistance and support on a particular topic (for example, New Zealand with police reform). Keep the internationals on tap, not on top. Of course, Australia is not the greatest villain that is the subject of this counter-analysis, just the greatest villain in the South Pacific. The United States is most criticised for this globally. What the Bougainvillean might say reflecting on Iraq, Afghanistan or Somalia is that the mistake in those places is allowing one international player to so dominate all others that if it loses the confidence of local factions, confidence in the entire peace process collapses. Demands grow for the international intervention to end before locals are ready to trust the credibility of one another's commitments without internationals standing beside them to support their commitments (Fortna 2008). The Bougainville experience would be that you need a separation of multiple international powers in peacebuilding to help locals design a coherent and legitimate separation of local powers.

Women and peacemaking

The best-known international strength of Bougainville's peacebuilding has been the engagement of individual women leaders in going out into the bush to persuade their young men to join the peace and organisations that have played a leadership role in peacebuilding such as the Bougainville Women for Peace and Freedom, the Bougainville Inter-Church Women's Forum and the Leitana Nehan Women's Development Agency (Saovana-Spriggs 2007:186–200; Sirivi and Havini 2004). Women's contributions to peace have not, however, been mirrored in the post-conflict political arrangements. Women argued for 12 reserved seats in the new *Constitution of an Autonomous Bougainville*, but achieved only three (Saovona-Spriggs 2007:106). In the 2005 election, the only women elected were to the three reserved seats—out of 41.

The strength of women's contributions to the peacebuilding is part of a wider pattern of the strengths of webs of civil-society contributions (Lederach 2005) by chiefs, churches and, more recently, youth leaders. There was impressive male leadership in these areas to match the female leadership. This strength at the bottom is not matched at the very top, where there has been limited work on reconciliations in Port Moresby, as discussed in the next section.

Feast and famine in state-building support

After armed conflict, humanitarian and development assistance tends to rush in as the peace descends and during the first few years of peace and then begins to dry up. This was very much the pattern in Bougainville, which was a flavour of the month at the end of the 1990s. Australian aid was maintained at the same absolute level of about $20 million a year throughout the first decade of the peace—coincidentally, about the same level it averaged per annum in military support for Papua New Guinea during the war. But the contributions of New Zealand and most other significant donors reduced greatly during the post-conflict years. The empirical evidence is that aid is more effective in the years after those first few years of peace, when absorption capacity is improved (Collier et al. 2003:175). This is so even though there is a good case for 'peace dividend' projects early on, which fund small projects with a quick dividend (rebuilding classrooms or repairing a bridge, for example) for communities that supported the peace process. The other side of this coin was the creation of expectations that could not be sustained that any 'good idea' for a peace-related project would cause money to flow and any 'good idea' for a workshop might deliver attendance fees for those who showed up.[2] One of the reasons for a gradual build-up of development assistance after some early peace dividend projects—as opposed to an early gush of support that dries up—is that early expectations might be created that while peace has dividends, those dividends are things locals must create and earn. The ABG today sometimes has problems getting citizen participation in a reform because it cannot afford to pay them. More fundamentally, it is a mistake to pay citizens to be active citizens because of the vast psychological evidence that extrinsic incentives crowd out intrinsic commitment (Frey and Jurgen 2000). For example, if you reward children with money for getting good marks at school, you crowd out their intrinsic commitment to education because they persuade themselves that the reason they study is for money. There are also dangers when inequalities between certain elites and have-nots are a source of the conflict that a steady flow of donor pay-offs to those same elites during peacebuilding can rekindle the resentments that fuelled the conflict (Regan 2005a).

---

2   UNPOB, the UNDP, Australia and New Zealand all paid allowances for attending peace meetings and awareness activities (Regan 2005a). Healthy attendances can make donors look good in the short term and are easy to justify when locals have no source of income.

Collier et al. (2003:177) also argue that another neglected strategy is strengthening technical capacity by financing the return of skilled members of the diaspora. This is not always true, however, in cases such as Afghanistan, where disasporas came in on fat contracts and returned to the West when their contracts ended. There is not a large Bougainvillean diaspora overseas, but across Papua New Guinea there is, especially in the civil service in Port Moresby, because of the superior education of Bougainvilleans historically. 'Levelling' elements of the BRA concerned about growing inequality in Bougainville also targeted many of the educated elite within Bougainville early in the war (Regan 2005b); many fled to new jobs on the mainland then and have never returned.

This was a long war during which schools were mostly destroyed and government services were withdrawn from the province for long periods. Indeed, there were years after the war ended when schools were not rebuilt or funded in the no-go zone. Basically a whole generation of Bougainvilleans missed out on an education during their childhood. Bougainville had benefited from a superior Marist education system during most of the twentieth century. Then it jumped further ahead of the rest of Papua New Guinea because of the large direct educational investment by BCL and the indirect investment as a result of Bougainville leaders using royalty income to improve education. It was the only PNG province that achieved universal primary school education in the 1980s (Regan 2007), though it did suffer from limited places in secondary schools. A huge compensatory adult education program to secure basics such as literacy and numeracy remains unfinished in Bougainville. The burnt-out main hospital in Bougainville, in Arawa, remains a slightly rebuilt shadow of what it once was (see generally Boege 2008).

Indigenous restorative justice

The weakness of the total collapse of the state in Bougainville created a space in which the strengths of traditional Bougainvillean reconciliation without police, courts and prisons could be revived and could shine (Boege 2006:10). The Bougainville Constitutional Commission put it this way:

> As Bougainville emerged from the long years of conflict there was no effective policing, almost no courts and no prisons. Notwithstanding that, Bougainville remains one of the safest communities in PNG. This is largely a credit to traditional chiefs and other traditional leaders who accepted the burden of maintaining a community based justice system during (and after) the conflict. (Quoted in Boege 2008:24)

The revival has not been easy in areas that had lost these traditions even before the war, and in some areas educated elites opposed the revival of traditions that would re-empower chiefs who they regarded as uneducated. One informant said reconciliation to solve problems without courts was building the kind of trust necessary for a small-scale village economy to get moving again. Post-conflict Bougainville is much more crime free than it was during the conflict and in the decade before the conflict. Indeed, it is one of the safest places in Papua New Guinea. Theft is particularly low in Bougainville, with damage or destruction of the property of parties believed to have caused a grievance being a bigger problem in the police statistics we saw than theft. Adultery, marriage break-up, land disputes, sorcery and 'false statements against another person' are each more common kinds of incidents that the police attend than common theft![3] That does not mean the country has returned to the extraordinarily crime-free society that it was in accounts from the 1960s and in the older anthropological literature. Home-brew—strong alcohol brewed from tropical fruits—is a scourge introduced as a result of the blockade (of beer) during the crisis that continues to inflict great damage on the social fabric. Home-brew contributes to domestic violence, which is universally observed to persist at a much higher level than was the case before the war.

Nevertheless, a 2004 victims-of-crime survey found low levels of crime in the two larger towns, Arawa and Buka, compared with other PNG urban centres. People were three times as likely to believe that crime had decreased than to believe it had increased in the past year (National Research Institute 2005). No incidents of killing were reported among the families of the 275 respondents and only one sexual assault. These results could have been much worse, however, had the survey been conducted further south in the Wisai area, where armed warlords were still clashing and there had been many murders in recent years. Siwai and Buin in the south and west are also high violence and homicide areas where serious progress on reconciliation of major schisms left over from the war among the likes of Damien Koike, Thomas Tari and Noah Musingku began seriously only after 2008. Violence there has been associated with these schisms and with the retention of large arsenals of weapons.

We asked many informants why there was so much rape during the war when Bougainville had been, according to the anthropological evidence, a society in which rape was extremely rare. The answer fairly consistently was that Bougainville was a society where the chiefs and female elders educated young men to respect women. The war allowed them to rebel against—even put themselves above—the authority of the chiefs, and order chiefs and female landowners around. Some commanders who wanted their boys to follow their authority also encouraged this; rape was sometimes a weapon in asserting their

---

3 Of course, families and chiefs deal with a great deal of petty stealing by children without involving the police. In the National Research Institute (2005:20) victims survey in both Arawa and Buka, 'alcohol or drug related crime' was by far the most common kind reported, with 'domestic violence' the second-most common in Arawa. In Buka, however, 'stealing' was reported much more frequently than 'domestic violence' as the number-two crime.

power. One strength of Bougainville peacebuilding was that these young men mostly were returned to the guidance of their chiefs and to habits of respecting women and listening to them. Rape and violence have fallen as a result, though domestic violence remains a huge problem among traumatised families. The police diagnosis of crime survey evidence is that crime has fallen most where traditional authority has been most effectively reasserted. Even when the war was at its worst, the moral code of respect could still break through to transform abuse. This is one mother's story from our interview notes:

> One of the BRA fighters let word out that he was going to take her daughter for himself. She was told he was coming with two other armed men. She arranged her nine children in a circle to pray with the targeted daughter beside her. The children said: 'What will we do?' Their mother said, 'Just think of Jesus.' When he [the BRA soldier] arrived, the mother greeted him in 'a spirit of Christian kindness', called him 'my son' with care in her voice. He said, 'I suppose you have heard that I want your daughter.' She said, 'My son. You think because there is no law and order you can take what you want. But there is law and order. It is in my heart and my children's hearts and it is there in your heart too. The war has not destroyed it in your heart.' He turned his gun upside down with the barrel grinding around and around in the earth, pensive. And said very well he will go and wished them peace. When the PNGDF attacked them two weeks later, this BRA man came around to warn them and help them pack up their most important things to make their escape. 'He was transformed.' (Fieldwork notes, Arawa, April 2006)

Still, there remains a warning sign in the will of young men to be in charge of chiefs during the war. Bougainville needs a youth policy and a bigger place in civil and political society for youth leaders. That worry was palpable on the roadblocks for years after the conflict ended, where many fourteen to sixteen year olds who had never fought in the war occupied a post-conflict spoiler niche.

Strengths and weaknesses in infrastructure support

The project funded by the Australian Government for upgrading and maintaining Bougainville's main trunk road, in which the international contractor is required to do the work by developing Bougainville maintenance teams and contractors along the route, has been moderately successful. The workforce for the project has mostly comprised hundreds, even thousands of ex-combatants over time, according to the contractor, to reintegrate them while building a sustainable local infrastructure upgrading and maintenance capacity. Yet trade will not fully flourish in Bougainville until many more bridges are rebuilt and the kind of coastal shipping service it enjoyed before the war is restored (Weeks 1999). While there has been some shocking waste and fraud in AusAID-funded combatant reintegration programs, we code this overall as a strength of the Bougainville peace in comparative terms. The Parliament of Bougainville is heavily populated by ex-combatants. Reconciliation ceremonies between Resistance and BRA fighters who have been brought together to form the majority of the Bougainville police have been remarkably successful. Men who once killed and tortured each other now seem to work together well without this past overwhelming them. One cannot expect a police force comprising men who often continue to suffer post-traumatic stress and who have completely missed out on their education to be one of the best one could find. But in all the circumstances of its history and composition, it is progressing well. Most ex-combatants have been successfully reintegrated into their old village economies, which are providing expanding opportunities for cash cropping of cocoa as well as subsistence agriculture.

Corruption

It is difficult to assess the level of corruption in Bougainville. Electoral Commission officials during the 2007 PNG elections saw vote buying in Bougainville, but much less than in the PNG Highlands. We were certainly told stories of corruption—some of quite serious concern at cabinet level. Money politics from foreign interests appears to be involved in a worrying way with access to Bougainville's valuable logging and fish resources. Still, we have coded corruption 'low' compared with other post-conflict cases. We accept PNG Police and National Intelligence Organisation informal assessments from 2006 and 2007 that corruption is less than in most of Papua New Guinea and less than in the Solomon Islands—in particular with less police corruption in Bougainville. Post-conflict, it is certainly less than we see today in the other regional cases of separatist wars: Aceh and West Papua.

Exemplary peacekeeping

The discipline of the TMG and PMG, their empowering of Bougainvilleans as the real players of the peace process, their displacement of rumour with quality information about the peace and their food and music were among a long list of strengths. The consensus Bougainvillean view that their only failing was not staying long enough, or not staying until the no-go zone was dismantled and the Me'ekamui weapons destroyed, is hard to evaluate. The reality is that President Kabui still had a respectful, if mutually distrustful, relationship with his fellow clansman from Panguna, Francis Ona, and he saw Ona's weapons as an insurance policy against Papua New Guinea refusing to honour the terms of the peace process. Sam Kauona shared this attitude. One commentator remarked that 'the MDF [Me'ekamui Defence Force] retaining weapons also became a reason (or excuse?) for the BRA and BRF [Resistance] to retain weapons, so as to ensure that the MDF did not have a monopoly of weaponry'. When Bougainville elites were interested in drawing out the full completion of weapons disposal over so many years, it was asking a lot to expect peacekeepers who were needed elsewhere in the world to hang in for so long. On the other hand, one commentator remarked that it was perhaps not a coincidence that the localised conflict in the south developed 'just after the UNOMB left'. A senior Australian intelligence official dissented from the Bougainville consensus: 'One reason Bougainville was such a successful peace operation was that our military was not allowed to become part of the problem. That was partly because they were not there for too long.' We then put it to him that armed roadblocks remained a major impediment to peace, trade and economic development (including tourism). We asked might it not have been better to keep a small, unarmed peacekeeping presence in Bougainville until locals negotiated the closure of the roadblocks. Then if local leaders persistently failed to close them, it would have been an option to move back a small contingent of, say, 60 armed peacekeepers to disarm the roadblocks. He replied:

> The military don't do things with 60 guys. [He went on to explain that just to keep one military helicopter in the air takes something approaching that number of people, especially on the logistics side.][4] External help often doesn't help. The CIA term is 'blowback'. Action so often produces an unpredictable reaction that makes things worse. Going in can complicate things for the locals. They ultimately have to work it out for themselves. It is risky for outsiders trying to resolve disputes among multiple big-men or warlords. As in Afghanistan, you don't understand well enough who is playing you off against who. You can exacerbate local problems. (Australian intelligence interview)

It is also hard to judge whether the failure of the Bougainville police to go in and arrest the young men on the roadblocks and to arrest Noah Musingku for his financial crimes (because Musingku's men are armed with M-16s) have been mistakes or another positive example of Melanesian patience in 'making peace by peaceful means' (ABG interview). The roadblocks are much less of a problem than they were. That does not mean they might not repeatedly come back in the context of the continuing law-enforcement vacuum when young men have guns. Well-armed police making arrests certainly sounds better than tacitly approving the breaking open of the containers with the weapons captured by the BRA at Kangu Beach, which then fall into the hands of Thomas Tari's Bougainville Freedom Fighters, who secretly pass some of those weapons on to local police

---

4   Our fieldwork notes on a similar question to an Australian general with Bougainville experience said: 'could not send in 50 military, but perhaps 50 armed police. It's bluff. They have to be willing to surrender their guns. If they run to the hills, you can't catch them in that country. Then they can just come down later.'

(without the formal approval of the President or the Police Commissioner—though probably with the tacit approval of the President)! Doing nothing with armed roadblocks is risky. All options are risky. Still, we accept this Australian intelligence assessment that local leaders will be in the best position to judge what options are least risky. One option local leaders will be best at assessing is whether they should be asking for international armed assistance to enforce the law against men with guns. Bougainville is in a trap of its own history here. It would be destabilising—and contrary to PNG Government policy—to have armed PNG forces come in to disarm roadblocks. And most of the people of Bougainville, including their President, are deeply committed to their police securing peace by peaceful means so they do not become like the PNG Police of 1988. But the paradox of state solicitation of peace by peaceful means is that states accomplish this more effectively when they are seen as controlling a monopoly of force that they are willing to use in extremis. Yet even without this image of invincibility, the ABG, by holding back on armed response in the final year of the Kabui presidency and during the Tanis presidency, has opened up spaces for reconciliations that are proceeding among the warring armed factions of the no-go zone and other areas of the south.

Figure 9.2 President Joseph Kabui pictured speaking at the Peacebuilding Conference organised by the Peacebuilding Compared project, the Buka Open Campus of the University of Papua New Guinea and the ABG on the occasion of the second anniversary of the ABG, June 2007

Photo: Leah Dunn

We have seen that these problems have in turn allowed a failure of law enforcement against financial crime—particularly by Noah Musingku. Micro-finance in Bougainville is crippled and is failing utterly to make the contribution it should be making to the economic redevelopment of the island.

Failure of international consensus building on honouring the referendum

A bigger weakness of peacebuilding in Bougainville has been the failure to build international consensus to honour the referendum that has been promised as part of a UN-sanctioned peace agreement. Regional leaders and diplomats in Australia, Indonesia and New Zealand and UN leaders in New York are showing zero leadership towards international pressure on Papua New Guinea that it must either persuade the people of Bougainville that they will be better off in Papua New Guinea or accept the consequences of the failure to persuade them. This preventive diplomacy to head off predictable conflict cries out to be done. With Port Moresby doing so little to persuade Bougainvilleans that they will be better off in Papua New Guinea, Bougainvilleans will be likely to vote for independence. Then if the PNG Parliament votes it down, guns could come out of boxes, guns could come back from the Solomon Islands and warlords could once again have a large following.

Delay in Bougainville consensus building on the future of the mine

A domestic consensus on how to manage the future of the mine is also an obstacle. There is considerable consensus within the Bougainville political elite that the mine should be opened to secure Bougainville's economic future. But there is also considerable opposition from the people, especially in Panguna and Central Bougainville generally. Among those who support opening the mine, there are those who think that it is better to go with BCL—'the devil we know'—which has the existing rights, and simply negotiate a better deal with them. Other members of the Bougainville elite have been picked off by Canadian, Chinese, Israeli, South African, Korean and Australian companies to seek their support for mine redevelopment. This poses a large risk to the integrity of the government. President Kabui received K20 000 from the Canadian company Invincible for his 2005 election campaign; in 2008, Kabui supported Invincible receiving a very broad mining licence. There are hugely divisive issues to settle here about which operator, if any, to choose, with what environmental controls, on how broad a lease, with what kind of local ownership, what kind of distribution of taxes and royalties between landowners and non-landowning Bougainvilleans. A more principled, transparent process was needed for putting the mining options to the people of Bougainville than that advanced by President Kabui's government. His successor as President, James Tanis, has been genuinely open to listening to the diverse and conflicting positions of his people in a new bottom-up attempt to forge a consensus on the future of the mine. This is a source of hope for the future of the country, particularly if the incoming president, John Momis, is able to build on this work in 2011.

A grand architecture of peace on humble foundations

Ultimately, peace in Bougainville came from a coalition of moderate Bougainvilleans from the BRA and supporters of Papua New Guinea, with early movers being village-level peacemakers on both sides, unifying an expanding coalition for peace. This coalition of moderates then negotiated as one for a compromise political settlement with Papua New Guinea.

Twelve years on, there have been no major violations of the Burnham truce and Lincoln cease-fire. As TMG Chief Negotiator, Rhys Puddicombe (2001:63), put the accomplishment, 'At that time [1997–98], I think all groups expected the truce to collapse, like previous cease-fires. Francis Ona was convinced that the peace process would fail without him.' There had been quite a history of previous peace initiatives. We count 11 pan-Bougainville peace initiatives discussed above (plus many local agreements—with the Buka leaders, in Selau, North Nasioi, for example) that had preceded Burnham I.

Like the peace in Aceh—which was another remarkable turnaround—in Bougainville, one of the striking things we have seen about the peace is how many people have made large contributions to it. One of those people who we have not singled out above is Colonel Bob Breen (2001a), then of the Australian Army. He makes the profound point for reluctant national contributors to peace operations that the experience of being a peacekeeper in Bougainville was a character-strengthening experience and a transformative life experience for many young Australians. The peace gave deeper meaning to the lives of many young Australians, New Zealanders, Fijians and ni-Vanuatu peace monitors who we interviewed. The Bougainville peace was not only good for Bougainville; it was good for Australia. Australia learnt important things from New Zealand in Bougainville. More fundamentally, it absorbed some of the peacebuilding character and courage from what New Zealanders would call the *mana* of many Bougainvillean women and men who lived peace in their being and their deeds. There were plenty of ruthless, exploitative Bougainville murderers as well, of course. Yet Australian hearts were also changed by seeing them brought to be something better through the fathomless spirituality of Bougainvillean reconciliation. Some will see this as a romantic reading. Peacebuilding is the avocation of romantics, as we see our attempt at a hard-edged analysis of Bougainville as documenting: romantics in harness with realist architects of transitional credible commitments.

An interesting aspect of post-conflict development in Bougainville has been some innovative thinking and incipient implementation of dual yet integrated models of traditional–modern governance and village–market economies. On the political front, we see this in the visionary governance designs of Theodore Miriung's Transitional Government. These have been neither strongly implemented nor extinguished by Miriung's successors. The essence of Miriung's vision was a kind of asymmetric constitutionalism within Bougainville in which some councils of elders would choose a governance hybrid that was more traditional and chiefly and others a hybrid more plural and democratic. But all councils of elders would valorise a kind of separation of powers—checks and balances between chiefly powers and the powers of electoral politics and rule of law. All councils of elders would foster the ideal of chiefs empowering democratic development and modern democracy empowering chiefs. The outcome desired was stronger traditional governance and stronger democratic governance. It was an example of cultural identity and cultural security through 'creative neotraditionalism' (Wanek 1996:311), indeed of hybrid political orders (Boege et al 2008). The danger Miriung sought to address was normlessness caused by the rule of the gun, which threatened both the traditional authority of male and female elders over young men and a democratic rule of law. For conquering that danger of normlessness, Miriung favoured whatever was the best kind of hybrid of traditional and modernising governance that would work best in a particular area.

President James Tanis worked with Miriung on that vision. He was part of a group of chiefs in Nagovis who supported a 'model village' that reinvigorated traditional authority and an economy based on reciprocity at the same time as it created spaces for those who wished to receive micro-finance to enter the market economy. The idea of the model village is that it strengthens opportunities for both kinds of economic flourishing side by side with a cultural flowering of traditional governance and democratic governance. The justice of the elders is a check and balance on abuse of power by militias and governments; the justice of democracy and courts and the ombudsman are checks and balances on abuse of power by chiefs as well as on corruption by politicians. Dual governance and a dual economy can knit and strengthen together. Whichever path an individual chooses, the village guarantees that they will never be allowed to go hungry, to live in poverty or be sent to prison.

The Bougainville peace is particularly instructive because of the virtuous circle that has been created between traditional bottom-up reconciliation and a distinctive kind of political settlement. The bottom-up reconciliation has been profoundly traditional. Yet in that Miriung spirit of hybridising traditional and modern virtues, Bougainvillean reconciliation has acquired some of its strength and resilience by laying itself open to a spirituality that Christianity delivered to it. That Christian influence also deepened the furrows of forgiveness in Bougainvillean traditional reconciliation. Women's church networks pushed women's wisdom to the forefront. Second, it laid itself open to modern thought and international experience on mediation, through the invitations to, for example, Leo White and Mark Plunkett in 1997 and to reflection on how New Zealand-style restorative justice principles and training might enhance traditional reconciliation through the agency of the Peace Foundation Melanesia (initially led by Brother Pat Howley, but from then on very Bougainvillean on the ground).

Bottom-up, village-by-village reconciliation created momentum for the top-down political settlement. That settlement then created a pacified space in which it was safe for local reconciliation to grow across all Bougainville. This was the virtuous circle between bottom-up reconciliation and top-down political settlement. The political settlement was innovative in its temporal sequencing of linked commitments that were made credible by the linkages. It took the form of 'we will do this when you are certified by the United Nations to have done that. When we have been certified to have done it, then and only then do we expect you to solve the next problem.' This temporal sequencing of linked commitments played out particularly in weapons disposal, power sharing and constitutional change. It meant a slow-food approach to a peace now tasted by the people of Bougainville (Boege 2006; Bowden et al. 2009).

Contemplating the limits of quantitative analysis

Bougainville is a good illustration of the limits of quantitative analyses of peace processes. We might code Bougainville as one successful negotiation at Lincoln University that secured peace. It was also a pattern of thousands of bottom-up local negotiations that were cumulatively successful. One at a time, these local reconciliations were very often unsuccessful (or successful at reconciling only actors who were peripheral to the local conflict). And in terms of top-down peace processes, we have coded 11 'unsuccessful' ones before the success from Burnham/Lincoln. So there are a very large number of peace process data points to make sense of within this 'one' case. Yet there is an analytical coherence to how we can code this nest of negotiations. The 'failed' Arawa Peace Conference of 1994 was in fact a limited success because it added to what the bottom-up local reconciliations were building towards the peace. But it and the 10 other peace processes that we conceive as 'failed' top-down peace processes were failures for the same reasons that the post-Burnham process was a success. These reasons are well captured by Barbara Walter's (2002) analysis of the 72 civil wars that started between 1940 and 1992. There was not enough of a hurting stalemate in Bougainville until 1997; at Arawa in 1994, elements of the PNGDF were still spoilers of their Prime Minister's push to peace—as was Francis Ona. By 1997, the costs of the war for all parties were—and appeared to all parties to be—much higher than at previous points during the long war.

In 1997, there was a third-party security guarantee that the parties would trust for the dangerous business of demobilising. In 1994, there had also been Operation Lagoon as third-party military guarantors of the peace process, but one side (the PNGDF) shot at both the peacekeepers and the BRA; and elements of the BRA, including their leader, Francis Ona, suspected that the Australian military was conspiring with the PNG Government to draw them into a trap to capture them (Breen 2001a). Bougainville is also consistent with Walter's (2002:22–3) theory that reciprocity in step-by-step demobilisation is needed, as explained by Robert Axelrod's (1984) *evolution of cooperation* (cooperation evolves tit for tat). That is, when one side sees the other side honour the first step of a commitment, it is more likely to honour the second. As a result, credible commitment grows cumulatively. Sequenced linked steps to demobilisation and disarmament were not committed to until the post-Lincoln process (Wolfers 2006a). Finally, also consistent with Walter's (2002) analysis, the post-Lincoln peace process succeeded where the previous 11 top-down attempts failed because it was the first to work through to credible guarantees of power sharing.[5] So, as with the hurting stalemate and credible third-party peacekeeper variables, so with the power-sharing variable, we in fact have 12 data points consistent with Walter's theory, not one.[6] The kind of summary coding in Table 9.1 abstracts too much from this qualitative–quantitative complexity.

---

5   Walter (2002:92) also finds that *in combination*, power sharing and third-party security guarantees are even more likely to secure lasting peace.
6   The Bougainville data points also fit Walter's (2002) empirical conclusion that an outside mediator helps peace processes get to the point of a signed agreement, but does not help them to become an implemented peace. The good offices of outside mediators such as Prime Ministers of the Solomon Islands helped deliver signed agreements, but before Lincoln did not deliver peacekeepers, sequenced commitments in the evolution of demobilisation, disarmament or power-sharing commitments. Consequently, they did not deliver peace.

10. Deep and shallow restorative peace

Table 10.1 tentatively characterises Bougainville as a 'restorative peace' rather than the much more common phenomena of a 'realist' or 'liberal peace'. A table like this might help us better see a conflict through a comparative lens, at the same time as it simplifies too much. Hence, in the conclusion to this chapter, we will reach the view that while Bougainville had a comparatively deep restorative peace locally, across the region that restorative peace was shallow. In particular, there remains a shallow regional reconciliation and a shallow integrity of regional truth on the question of honouring the outcome of the forthcoming referendum on independence for Bougainville.

Table 10.2 characterises Bougainville as bottom-up for truth and reconciliation, which again is quite unusual compared with very common war settlements of non-truth and top-down reconciliation. Bougainville had no top-down truth commission such as we have seen in various Latin American countries, or a South African-style Truth and Reconciliation Commission. So we see Bougainville as a case of deep bottom-up reconciliation and shallow regional truth. Regional elites in Port Moresby, Canberra, Wellington and Jakarta and in the boardroom of BCL now have obligations to enliven the integrity of regional dialogue about the Bougainville peace agreement.

Table 10.1 Accomplishing peace through political settlement, legal justice and restorative justice

How peace is accomplished	Political settlement	Adjudicated wrongdoing based on legal justice	Reconciliation of wrongdoing based on restorative justice/traditional reconciliation	Provisional interpretation
Unresolved conflict Burma	No	No	No	Hobbesian struggle
Political settlement ignoring war crimes Korea	Yes	No	No	Realist peace
Political settlement and rule of law Nazi Germany	Yes	Yes	No	Liberal peace
Political settlement and reconciliation Bougainville	Yes	No	Yes	Restorative peace
Political settlement, rule of law and reconciliation Attempted in Timor-Leste and South Africa	Yes	Yes	Yes	Republican peace*
Pure rule of law Hard to identify a clear case	No	Yes	No	Peace by rule of international law
Rule of law and reconciliation Hard to identify a clear case	No	Yes	Yes	Peace by restorative international law
Pure reconciliation Hard to identify; some preventive diplomacy could approach it	No	No	Yes	Restorative peace without political settlement

* Barnett's (2006) concept of republican peace would require of the political settlement that it include commitment to a constitution with a separation of powers and that the settlement be based on deliberative politics that is broadly representative.

Table 10.2 Variation in how bottom-up and top-down are truth and reconciliation*

How peace is accomplished	Bottom-up truth	Top-down truth	Bottom-up reconciliation	Top-down reconciliation	Provisional interpretation
Bottom-up truth and reconciliation Bougainville	Yes	No	Yes	No	Truthful local reconciliations
Top-down truth and non-reconciliation Chile**	No	Yes	No	No	Pure Truth Commission model
Top-down truth and reconciliation South Africa***	No	Yes	No	Yes	National Truth and Reconciliation Commission model
Truth and reconciliation bottom-up–top-down Timor-Leste (short-term attempt at it)	Yes	Yes	Yes	Yes	National and local Truth and Reconciliation Commission
Non-truth and non-reconciliation World War I	No	No	No	No	Feigned forgetting
Non-truth and reconciliation Poso (Braithwaite et al. 2010)	No	No	Yes	Yes	Forgive and forget
Truth and non-reconciliation Korean War	Yes	Yes	No	No	Remember and resent
Non-truth and top-down reconciliation Tito's communist Yugoslavia	No	No	No	Yes	Feigned forgetting, elites forgive (but hatred hides in people's hearts)

* This table lists only half the combinations of the four columns possible for these variables. We expect some of the hidden combinations will be brought to life as Peacebuilding Compared accumulates new cases.

** There was some bottom-up truth in Chile from NGOs, though nothing like the breadth of local bottom-up truth in Bougainville.

*** There were some important attempts at bottom-up truth and reconciliation in South Africa as well that were not widely based.

The bottom-up truth and reconciliations in Bougainville have been quite different from those we described for a number of Indonesian conflicts in the first volume of Peacebuilding Compared (Braithwaite et al. 2010). We described these as cases of non-truth and reconciliation. Much of that Indonesian reconciliation was real enough, but based on no-one making explicit admissions of wrongdoing and apologising for it. In contrast, reconciliations within Bougainville—while slow getting to the point of admissions—have been strong on both admission of specific wrongdoing, even for murder and rape, and marking that by the payment of traditional compensation or heartfelt apology, reciprocated by (mostly) binding forgiveness. One leading Bougainville woman said the philosophy was 'if you don't reconcile, don't talk to each other' because interaction without reconciliation could lead to violence. In contrast, Indonesian non-truth and reconciliation were based on adversaries working together on rebuilding and reintegration projects without ever admitting to wrongdoing. Over the next 20 years of this project, we will follow the ways such different dispensations succeed and fail in the resilience of peace. But for the moment, Tables 10.1 and 10.2 do no more than float only provisional interpretations (as opposed to variables we code) in the hope they might provoke conversations to clarify and elaborate them. We hope the project will have a wiki quality with a conceptual architecture that will be adjusted as new cases are added.

This is a book on the particularities of Bougainville's war and peace. It is not the place for exegesis on what is theoretically at stake down the right-hand columns of Tables 10.1 and 10.2. That in any case is better refined from the experience of more cases followed up for longer. For the moment, these tables help us to see how distinctive the Bougainville peace was and the way it was distinctive. And really, that is the only claim we advance for Tables 10.1 and 10.2 at this early stage of our comparative project. Doubtless we could end up concluding that Tables 10.1 and 10.2 are too reductively simple for any wider purpose. Needless to say, however, it is a firm conclusion that the Bougainville peace has been remarkable because of the distinctive strengths of its expanding webs of traditional bottom-up reconciliation and the architectural supports of its political settlement.

The fact that it is hard to find clear cases for the last three rows of Table 10.1 at this stage of Peacebuilding Compared—cases where peace has been secured by legal justice or reconciliation without a political settlement—could signal an important caution to our analysis. Without a political settlement to a war, it could be that bottom-up reconciliation will always be crushed by future waves of conflict. That does not imply a political settlement must always come first. The Bougainville case shows that bottom-up reconciliation achieves only fragile progress when war rages around it. Yet we also find that early reconciliations paved the way to a political settlement. So we hypothesise that the commonly expressed wisdom during our fieldwork in the corridors of the United Nations in New York that 'peacekeeping cannot work if there is no peace to keep' goes too far. While a political settlement can create peace without genuine truth and reconciliation, and while truth and reconciliation might be unlikely to secure peace without a political settlement, truth, justice and reconciliation could be more than just value added on top of a settlement. Rather, we hypothesise that top-down political settlement and bottom-up restorative justice form a virtuous circle that consolidates deeply sustainable peace. PMG Commander Brigadier Bruce Osborn's metaphor was of the peace as building a house that acquired strong foundations because of traditional reconciliation and sturdy walls because of the architecture of the peace: 'The foundations of the house were the Bougainvillean people. The walls were the various parties to the peace process. You had to shape, strengthen and unify those walls in order to support the roof, which was the reconciliation government, the one voice of Bougainville' (Osborn 2001:55).

While Bougainvilleans identified with and built Brigadier Osborn's house, they now have the space to contemplate whether it could be better buttressed by some national and international architecture. Simply because local reconciliation continues to progress reasonably well, gradually expanding its scope within Bougainville, it does not necessarily follow that a National Truth and Reconciliation Commission on the Bougainville war would be redundant for Papua New Guinea. Some PNGDF soldiers and riot police we interviewed benefited from participating in local reconciliations that occurred in 1991 and also from reconciliations between the Lincoln cease-fire and the departure of the last PNGDF in April 2003. But most PNGDF and riot police were not on the ground at those times and places and participated in no reconciliations with the people of Bougainville. In one of our interviews with two members of the Police Mobile Squad in Port Moresby, they said they felt for their colleagues who had married Bougainville women and had children living on the mainland, or who had left a Bougainville wife and children behind, when those children would benefit from reconciliation and connection with their mother's or their father's family. They also expressed this concern for orphaned Bougainvillean children who had been adopted by PNG police and soldiers. Then they mentioned the unreconciled state of PNG police and soldiers who defected to the BRA after landing in Bougainville and others who defected in the other direction who were still serving in the police or military on the mainland today.

No national reconciliation ceremony was ever conducted for the Bougainville war in Port Moresby. The Bougainville Women for Peace and Freedom had considered reaching out to the PNGDF with a 'Where's my son movement', given the importance in Bougainville of returning the bones of the fallen. Nothing organised has come of this. Many Bougainvilleans living in Port Moresby, and other parts of Papua New Guinea, were violently victimised during the war. About 15 000 refugees who fled to the mainland from Bougainville have not experienced reconciliation concerning the loss of jobs and homes and harassment they suffered. None of the Chinese refugees who had lived in Bougainville's Chinatowns for generations experienced reconciliation for the loss of their homes, businesses and the disappearance from history's page of the entire little communities they had eked out in Bougainville. They have their story of oppression to tell as indentured 'coolie' labour of the Germans, chased out twice in the next two generations—by the Japanese and then by Bougainvilleans. Young Bougainvilleans today have little comprehension of their truth. BCL and its old and current expatriate management would benefit from a reconciliation process with a Bougainville that must come to terms with the fact that these expatriates still have legal title to mining rights in their lands. That might be difficult while BCL is afraid of the legal implications of apologising. In any case, there it would be perhaps more meaningful for the Australian Government to apologise for the mine, its support for the war in its early years, and more. One argument some Bougainville leaders advance against a Truth and Reconciliation Commission is that it is an alien institution for Bougainville society. This is not much of an argument against its application with alienated aliens to Bougainville society. This is not to deny that it is equally an option to embrace these aliens within traditional Bougainvillean reconciliation. That embrace might spiritually enrich them.

Our interviews on the mainland revealed a lot of 'forgive and forget' attitudes, but also some residual bitterness in these quarters. Healing is important not only to these damaged people. It is also in the interests of a secure relationship for Bougainville with Papua New Guinea. A National Truth and Reconciliation Commission might give former PNG leaders and Australian leaders a space in which to apologise for the mistakes they made between the 1960s and Sandline. The need even more profound than reconciliation in Port Moresby is for a truth of greater integrity. For many in the PNG political elite, there is no truth to the commitment to honour the will that the people of Bougainville were empowered to express through an independence referendum. For these PNG politicians, it was a trick, not a truth, and that was why there was no legally binding undertaking to honour the outcome of that vote. ABG leaders such as the one who said 'some people were not genuine when they signed the peace agreement' and who accused the Prime Minister, Sir Michael Somare, of being one of those less than genuine leaders,[1] are hardly blind to the prospect of betrayal. Those in

---

1 Some insiders in Port Moresby we interviewed said quite the opposite of Sir Michael's good faith on Bougainville. One said, 'Sir Michael Somare has repeatedly stated in public that his government is committed to honouring the letter and spirit of the *Bougainville Peace Agreement* and implementing laws.'

the Port Moresby elite who think it would be wrong under any circumstance to allow the break-up of Papua New Guinea have many who agree with them in the capitals of the regional powers: Canberra, Jakarta and Wellington.

There is a need for a regional conversation on the integrity of the national and international buttressing of the Bougainville peace process. A National Truth and Reconciliation Commission is not the only way to accomplish that, of course. The Prime Ministers of Papua New Guinea, Australia and New Zealand simply issuing statements that they personally support honouring the wishes that the people of Bougainville vote for (while expressing the hope they vote to stay in Papua New Guinea) could be a significant step towards securing enduring peace. Australian diplomats persuaded Bougainvilleans to agree to their plan of a delayed referendum by saying Australia would organise international diplomatic pressure on Port Moresby to honour the referendum result. This was not unlike the way Australia in that period pressured Jakarta to honour the 1999 East Timor referendum. New Zealand diplomats were also unusually involved in that pressure on Jakarta over the East Timor referendum. So Wellington could also say that the international community must demand that the wishes of the people of Bougainville as expressed in the referendum are honoured. Jakarta could help by saying it did honour the East Timor referendum, and likewise Port Moresby should honour the Bougainville peace agreement.

Appendix

Numbers and types of people interviewed, Bougainville case

Elected Official (PNG and Bougainville)	15
Civil Servant (PNG and Bougainville)	27
Political leader of oppositional group	2
PNG Security Forces Combatant in Bougainville	9
BRA Combatant	18
Resistance Combatant	13
Me'ekamui Defence Force	7
TMG/PMG/Operation Lagoon Peacekeeper: Australia	29
TMG/PMG/Operation Lagoon Peacekeeper: New Zealand	18
TMG/PMG/Operation Lagoon Peacekeeper: Vanuatu	12
TMG/PMG/Operation Lagoon Peacekeeper: Fiji	6
Bougainville Police (most also ex-combatants)	19
Chief/Indigenous/Village Leader	16
Religious leader	10
Women's NGO	11
Environmental NGO	0
Development NGO	10
Human Rights/Peacebuilding NGO	13
Other NGO	0
Journalist	1
Business leader	10
Student/youth leader	3
Foreign Govt (Ambassador, Foreign Minister of another country, USAID etc)	16
International Organizations	5
Researcher/university academic	2
Victim/IDP	4
Other	0
Total interviews	248
Total people interviewed	276

References

Ahai, Naihuwo Garry 1999 'Grassroots development visions for a new Bougainville', in Geoff Harris, Naihuwo Ahai and Rebecca Spence (eds), *Building Peace in Bougainville*, Armidale, NSW, and Waigani, PNG: The Centre for Peace Studies, University of New England and National Research Institute.

Alpers, Philip 2005 *Gun-running in Papua New Guinea: from arrows to assault weapons in the Southern Highlands*, Special Report, Geneva: Small Arms Survey.

Amnesty International 1997 *Papua New Guinea, Bougainville: The forgotten human rights tragedy*, London: Amnesty International.

Axelrod, Robert 1984 *The Evolution of Cooperation*, New York: Basic Books.

Barnett, Michael 2006 'Building a republican peace: stabilizing states after war', *International Security* 30(4), 87–112.

Boege, Volker 2006 *Bougainville and the discovery of slowness: an unhurried approach to state-building in the Pacific*, Occasional Paper Series No. 3, Brisbane: The Australian Centre for Peace and Conflict Studies.

Boege, Volker 2008 *A promising liaison: kastom and state in Bougainville*, Occasional Paper Series No. 12, Brisbane: The Australian Centre for Peace and Conflict Studies.

Boege, Volker, Anne Brown, Kevin Clements and Anna Nolan 2008 *On hybrid political orders and emerging states: state formation in the context of' 'fragility'*, Germany: Berghof Center for Constructive conflict Management.

Boutros-Ghali, Boutros 1995 *An Agenda for Peace*, Second edition, New York: United Nations.

Bowden, Brett, Hilary Charlesworth and Jeremy Farrall 2009 'Introduction', in B. Bowden, H. Charlesworth and J. Farrall (eds), *The Role of International Law in Rebuilding Societies After Conflict*, Cambridge, UK: Cambridge University Press.

Braithwaite, John 2002 *Restorative Justice and Responsive Regulation*, New York and Sydney: Oxford University Press and Federation Press.

Braithwaite, John, Valerie Braithwaite, Michael Cookson and Leah Dunn 2010 *Anomie and Violence: Non-truth and reconciliation in Indonesian peacebuilding*, Canberra: ANU E Press.

Braithwaite, Valerie 2009 *Defiance in Taxation and Governance: Resisting and dismissing authority in a democracy*, Cheltenham, UK: Edward Elgar.

Breen, Bob 2001a *Giving Peace a Chance: Operation Lagoon, Bougainville 1994: a case of military action and diplomacy*, Canberra: Strategic Defence Studies, The Australian National University.

Breen, Bob 2001b 'Coordinating monitoring and defence support', in Monica Wehner and Donald Denoon (eds), *Without a Gun: Australians' experiences monitoring peace in Bougainville, 1997–2001*, Canberra: Pandanus Books.

Brown, M. J. F. 1974 'A development consequence—disposal of mining waste on Bougainville, Papua New Guinea', *Geoforum* 18, 19–27.

Carruthers, D. S. 1990 'Some implications for Papua New Guinea of the closure of the Bougainville copper mine', in Ronald James May and Matthew Spriggs (eds), *The Bougainville Crisis*, Bathurst, NSW: Crawford House Press.

Charlesworth, Hilary 2008 'Are women peaceful? Reflections on the role of women in peace building', *Feminist Legal Studies* 16, 347–61.

Claxton, Karl 1998 *Bougainville 1988–98: Five searches for security in the North Solomons province of Papua New Guinea*, Canberra: Strategic and Defence Studies Centre.

Collier, Paul 2007 *The Bottom Billion: Why the poorest countries are failing and what can be done about it*, Oxford: Oxford University Press.

Collier, Paul, V. L Elliott, Hårvard Hegre, Anke Hoeffler, Marta Reynal-Querol and Nicholas Sambanis 2003 *Breaking the Conflict Trap: Civil war and development policy*, Washington, DC: The World Bank and Oxford University Press.

Denoon, Donald 2000 *Getting Under the Skin: The Bougainville copper agreement and the creation of the Panguna Mine*, Carlton, Vic.: Melbourne University Press.

Dinnen, Sinclair and John Braithwaite 2009 'Reinventing policing through the prism of the colonial kiap', *Policing and Society* 19(2), 161–73.

Dinnen, Sinclair, Ron May and Anthony J. Regan (eds) 1997 *Challenging the State: The Sandline affair in Papua New Guinea*, Canberra: Department of Political and Social Change, The Australian National University.

Dorney, Sean 1998 *The Sandline Affair: Politics and mercenaries and the Bougainville crisis*, Sydney: ABC Books.

Dove, J., T. Miriung and M. Togolo 1974 'Mining bitterness', in Peter G. Sack (ed.), *Problem of Choice: Land in Papua New Guinea's future*, Canberra: The Australian National University Press.

Downer, Alexander 2001 *The Bougainville Crisis: An Australian perspective*, Canberra: Department of Foreign Affairs and Trade.

Eagles, Julie 2002 'Aid as an instrument for peace: a civil society perspective', *Conciliation Resources*, viewed 2 July 2007, <www.c-r.org/our-work/accord/png-bougainville/aid.php>

Elder, Peter 2005 'Between the waitman's wars: 1914–42', in Anthony J. Regan and Helga M. Griffin (eds), *Bougainville Before the Conflict*, Canberra: Pandanus Books.

Evans, Lissa 1992 'The health and social situation on Bougainville', in Matthew Spriggs and Donald Denoon (eds), *The Bougainville Crisis: 1991 update*, Bathurst, NSW: Crawford House Press.

Filer, Colin 1992 'The escalation of disintegration and the reinvention of authority', in Matthew Spriggs and Donald Denoon (eds), *The Bougainville Crisis: 1991 update*, Bathurst, NSW: Crawford House Press.

Fortna, Virginia P. 2008 *Does Peacekeeping Work? Shaping belligerents' choices after civil war*, Princeton, NJ: Princeton University Press.

Fraenkel, Jon 2004 *The Manipulation of Custom: From uprising to intervention in the Solomon Islands*, Wellington, NZ: Victoria University Press.

Frey, Bruno and Reto Jurgen 2000 *Motivation crowding theory: a survey of empirical evidence*, SSRN Working Paper, viewed 22 May 2009, <papers.ssrn.com/sol3/papers.cfm?abstract_id=203330>

Gillespie, Rosemarie 1999 *Ecocide*, Lyneham, ACT: Me'ekamui Publications.

Gillespie, Rosemarie 2009 *Running with Rebels: Behind the lies in Bougainville's hidden war*, Australia: Ginibi Publications.

Gladwell, Malcolm 2002 *The Tipping Point*, New York: Little Brown.

Griffin, James 1990 'Bougainville is a special case', in Ronald James May and Matthew Spriggs (eds), *The Bougainville Crisis*, Bathurst, NSW: Crawford House Press.

Griffin, James 2005 'Movements towards secession 1964–76', in Anthony J. Regan and Helga M. Griffin (eds), *Bougainville Before the Conflict*, Canberra: Pandanus Books.

Havini, Moses 1992 'A Bougainvillean perspective on the crisis', in Matthew Spriggs and Donald Denoon (eds), *The Bougainville Crisis: 1991 update*, Bathurst, NSW: Crawford House Press.

Havini, Moses 1999 *Bougainville: The long struggle for freedom*, Sydney: New Age Publishers.

Hermkens, Anna-Karina 2007 'Religion in war and peace: unravelling Mary's intervention in the Bougainville crisis', *Culture and Religion* 8(3), 271–89.

Hilson, Christopher J. 2007 'Mining and civil conflict: revisiting grievance at Bougainville', *Minerals & Energy—Raw Materials Report* 21(2), 23–35.

Howley, Patrick n.d. Unpublished document, Port Moresby: Peace Foundation Melanesia.

Howley, Patrick 2000 *Restorative Justice in Bougainville*, Canberra: State, Society and Governance in Melanesia Project, The Australian National University.

Howley, Patrick 2002 *Breaking Spears and Mending Hearts*, London and Sydney: Zed Books and The Federation Press.

Independent State of Papua New Guinea 1990 *Crisis in the North Solomons Province: Report of the Special Committee appointed by the National Executive Council*, Port Moresby.

Job, Jenny and Monica Reinhart 2003 'Trust the tax office: does Putnam's thesis relate to tax?', *Australian Journal of Social Issues* 38(3), 307–34.

Joint Standing Committee on Foreign Affairs, Defence and Trade 2005 *Bougainville: The peace process and beyond*, Canberra: Parliament of Australia.

Kaldor, Mary 1999 *New and Old Wars: Organized violence in a global era*, Stanford, Calif.: Stanford University Press.

Kauona, Sam 2001 'Freedom from fear', in Rebecca Adams (ed.), *Peace on Bougainville: Truce Monitoring Group Gudpel Nius Bilong Peace*, Wellington, NZ: Victoria University Press.

Kemelfield, Graeme 1990 'A short history of the Bougainville ceasefire', in Ronald James May and Matthew Spriggs (eds), *The Bougainville Crisis*, Bathurst, NSW: Crawford House Press.

Kemelfield, Graeme 1992 'Reflections on the Bougainville conflict: underlying causes and conditions for a resolution', in Matthew Spriggs and Donald Denoon (eds), *The Bougainville Crisis: 1991 update*, Bathurst, NSW: Crawford House Press.

Kenneth, Roselyne 2005 'Land for agriculture—silent women: men's voices', in Anthony J. Regan and Helga M. Griffin (eds), *Bougainville Before the Conflict*, Canberra: Pandanus Books.

Lawrence, Peter 1964 *Road Belong Cargo: A study of the cargo movement in the southern Madang District New Guinea*, Manchester: Manchester University Press.

Lederach, John Paul 1997 *Building Peace: Sustainable reconciliation in divided societies*, Washington, DC: US Institute of Peace.

Lederach, John Paul 2005 *The Moral Imagination: The art and soul of building peace*, Oxford: Oxford University Press.

Liria, Yauka A. 1993 *Bougainville Campaign Diary*, Victoria: Indra Publishing.

Londey, Peter 2004 *Other People's Wars: A history of Australian peacekeeping*, Crows Nest, NSW: Allen & Unwin.

Lumanni, Joachim 2005 'Post-1960s cocoa and copra production in Bougainville', in Anthony J. Regan and Helga M. Griffin (eds), *Bougainville Before the Conflict*, Canberra: Pandanus Books.

Marino, Pascal 2006 'Beyond economic benefits: the contribution of microfinance to post-conflict recovery in Asia and the Pacific', in Matthew Clarke (ed.), *Aid in Conflict*, New York: Nova Science Publishers.

Matthew, Anthony 2000 'Bougainville and Papua New Guinea: complexities of secession in a multi-ethnic developing state', *Political Studies* 48, 724–44.

May, Ronald James 1990 'Political implications of the Bougainville crisis', in Ronald James May and Matthew Spriggs (eds), *The Bougainville Crisis*, Bathurst, NSW: Crawford House Press.

Momis, John Lawrence 2005 'Shaping leadership through Bougainville indigenous values and Catholic seminary training—a personal journey', in Anthony J. Regan and Helga M. Griffin (eds), *Bougainville Before the Conflict*, Canberra: Pandanus Books.

Moulik, T. K. 1977 *Bougainville in Transition*, Canberra: Development Studies Centre, The Australian National University.

Nash, Jill and Eugene Ogan 1990 'The red and the black: Bougainvillean perceptions of other Papua New Guineans', *Pacific Studies* 13(2) (March), 1–17.

National Research Institute 2005 *Community Crime Survey*, Waigani, PNG: National Research Institute.

Nelson, Hank 2005 'Bougainville in World War II', in Anthony J. Regan and Helga M. Griffin (eds), *Bougainville Before the Conflict*, Canberra: Pandanus Books.

Neustadt, Richard E. and Ernest R. May 1986 *Thinking in Time: The uses of history for decision-makers*, New York: Free Press.

Newsom, John 2002 'Bougainville microfinance: rebuilding rural communities after the crisis', *Development Bulletin* 52, 85–8.

Ninnes, Peter 2006 'Non-government organisations, peacebuilding and global networks', in Helen Hakena, Peter Ninnes and Bert Jenkins (eds), *NGOs and Post Conflict Recovery: The Leitana Nehan Women's Development Agency, Bougainville*, Canberra: Asia Pacific Press and ANU E Press.

O'Callaghan, Mary-Louise 1999 *Enemies Within: Papua New Guinea, Australia, and the Sandline crisis. The inside story*, Sydney: Doubleday.

Ogan, Eugene 1972 'Business and cargo: socio-economic change among the Nasioi of Bougainville', *New Guinea Research Bulletin* No. 44, Port Moresby and Canberra: The New Guinea Research Unit, The Australian National University.

Ogan, Eugene 1990 'Perspectives on a crisis (5)', in Peter Polomka (ed.), *Bougainville: perspectives on a crisis*, Canberra Papers on Strategy and Defence No. 66, Canberra: Strategic and Defence Studies Centre, The Australian National University.

Okole, Henry 1990 'The politics of the Panguna landowners' organization', in Ronald James May and Matthew Spriggs (eds), *The Bougainville Crisis*, Bathurst, NSW: Crawford House Press.

Oliver, Douglas 1955 *A Solomon Island Society: Kinship and leadership among the Siuai of Bougainville*, Cambridge, Mass.: Harvard University Press.

Oliver, Douglas 1973 *Bougainville: A personal history*, Victoria: Melbourne University Press.

Oliver, Douglas 1991 *Black Islanders: A personal perspective of Bougainville 1937–1991*, Honolulu: University of Hawai'i Press.

Osborn, Bruce 2001 'The role of the military commander', in Monica Wehner and Donald Denoon (eds), *Without a Gun: Australians' experiences monitoring peace in Bougainville, 1997–2001,* Canberra: Pandanus Books.

Percy, Sarah 2007 *Mercenaries: The history of a norm in international relations,* Oxford: Oxford University Press.

Pettit, Philip 1997 *Republicanism: A theory of freedom and government,* Oxford: Oxford University Press.

Puddicombe, Rhys 2001 'Role of the chief negotiator', in Monica Wehner and Donald Denoon (eds), *Without a Gun: Australians' experiences monitoring peace in Bougainville, 1997–2001,* Canberra: Pandanus Books.

Reddy, Peter 2006 Peace operations and restorative justice: groundwork for post-conflict regeneration, PhD dissertation, Canberra: The Australian National University.

Regan, Anthony 1999 Submission to the Foreign Affairs Sub-Committee of the Joint Standing Committee on Foreign Affairs, Defence and Trade Inquiry: Bougainville: The peace process and beyond, Parliament of Australia.

Regan, Anthony 2000 '"Traditional" leaders and conflict resolution in Bougainville', in Sinclair Dinnen and Allison Ley (eds), *Reflections on Violence in Melanesia,* Sydney: Hawkins Press.

Regan, Anthony 2001 'Why a neutral peace monitoring force', in Monica Wehner and Donald Denoon (eds), *Without a Gun: Australians' experiences monitoring peace in Bougainville 1997–2001,* Canberra: Pandanus Books.

Regan, Anthony 2002a 'Bougainville: beyond survival', *Cultural Survival Quarterly* 26(3).

Regan, Anthony 2002b 'The Bougainville political settlement and the prospects for sustainable peace', *Pacific Economic Bulletin* 17(1), 114–29.

Regan, Anthony 2002c 'Resolving two dimensions of conflict: the dynamics of consent, consensus and compromise', *Conciliation Resources,* viewed 2 July 2007, <www.c-r.org/our-work/accord/png-bougainville/resolving.php>

Regan, Anthony 2003 'The Bougainville conflict: political and economic agendas', in Karen Ballentine and Jake Sherman (eds), *The Political Economy of Armed Conflict: Beyond greed and grievance,* Boulder, Colo.: Lynne Rienner.

Regan, Anthony 2005a Doing less to achieve more: 'lessons' from a successful international peacebuilding intervention—Bougainville 1997–200, Canberra: Australian National University. , Draft paper for Regan (2010).

Regan, Anthony 2005b Autonomy and conflict resolution: three autonomies in Bougainville, Papua New Guinea, 1976–2005, Paper presented to Comparative National Experiences of Autonomy: Purpose, Structures and Institutions Conference, University of Hong Kong.

Regan, Anthony 2005c 'Identities among Bougainvilleans', in Anthony J. Regan and Helga M. Griffin (eds), *Bougainville Before the Conflict*, Canberra: Pandanus Books.

Regan, Anthony 2007 'Development and conflict: the struggle for self-determination in Bougainville', in Anne M. Brown (ed.), *Security and Development in the Pacific Islands: Social resilience in emerging states*, Boulder, Colo.: Lynne Rienner.

Regan, Anthony 2008 'Sustainability of international peace-building interventions—the Bougainville experience, 1997–2006', in Greg Fry and Tarcisius Tara Kabutaulaka (eds), *Intervention and State-Building in the Pacific*, Manchester: Manchester University Press.

Regan, Anthony 2010 *Light Intervention: Lessons from Bougainville*, Washington, DC: US Institute of Peace Press.

Rimoldi, Max and Eleanor Rimoldi 1992 *Hahalis and the Labour of Love: A social movement on Buka Island*, Providence, RI, and Oxford, UK: Berg Publishers.

Rolfe, Jim 2001 'Peacekeeping the pacific way in Bougainville', *International Peacekeeping* 8(4), 38–55.

Ross, Michael L. 2004 'How do natural resources influence civil war? Evidence from thirteen cases', *International Organization* 58, 35–67.

Rudé, George F. E. 1964 *The Crowd in History: A study of popular disturbances in France and England, 1730–1848*, London: Lawrence and Wishart.

Saovana-Spriggs, Ruth V. 2007 Gender and peace: Bougainvillean women, matriliny, and the peace process, PhD dissertation, The Australian National University, Canberra.

Scheye, Eric and Gordon Peake 2005 'Unknotting local leadership', in Anja Ebnöther and Philipp H. Fluri (eds), *After Intervention: Public security management in post-conflict societies. From intervention to sustainable local ownership*, Vienna and Geneva: Bureau for Security Policy at the Austrian Ministry of Defence and Geneva Centre for Democratic Control of Armed Forces.

Sharp, Naomi 1997 *Bougainville: Blood on our hands*, Woollahra, NSW: Aid Watch.

Shaw, Judith and Matthew Clarke 2004 Risky business in Bougainville: implementing microfinance in post-conflict environment, Paper presented to Conference on Making Peace Work, Helenski.

Shearing, Clifford 1997 'Violence and the changing face of governance: privatization and its implications', *Kolner Zeitschrift fur Soziologie und Sozialpsychologie*.

Sirivi, Josephine Tankunani and Marilyn Taleo Havini (eds) 2004 *As Mothers of the Land: The birth of the Bougainville Women for Peace and Freedom*, Canberra: Pandanus Books.

Spark, Natascha and Jackie Bailey 2005 'Disarmament in Bougainville: "guns in boxes"', *International Peacekeeping* 12(4) (Winter), 599–608.

Spriggs, Matthew 1992 'Bougainville update: August 1990 to May 1991', in M. Spriggs and D. Denoon (eds), *The Bougainville Crisis: 1991 update*, Bathurst, NSW: Crawford House Press.

Spriggs, Matthew 2005 'Bougainville's early history: an archaeological perspective', in Anthony J. Regan and Helga M. Griffin (eds), *Bougainville Before the Conflict*, Canberra: Pandanus Books.

Stedman, Stephen J. 1997 'Spoiler problems in peace processes', *International Security* 22(2), 5–53.

Tanis, James 2002a 'Reconciliation: my side of the island', *Conciliation Resources*, viewed 2 July 2007, <www.c-r.org/our-work/accord/png-bougainville/reconciliation.php>

Tanis, James 2002b *In between: personal experiences in the 9-year long conflict on Bougainville*, State, Society and Governance in Melanesia Project Working Paper, Canberra: The Australian National University.

Togolo, Melchior 2005 'Torau response to change', in Anthony J. Regan and Helga M. Griffin (eds), *Bougainville Before the Conflict*, Canberra: Pandanus Books.

Tonissen, Michelle 2000 'The relationship between development and violence against women in post-conflict Bougainville', *Development Bulletin* 53, 26–8.

Tryon, Darrell 2005 'The languages of Bougainville', in Anthony J. Regan and Helga M. Griffin (eds), *Bougainville Before the Conflict*, Canberra: Pandanus Books.

UNIFEM 2004 *Getting it Right, Doing it Right: Gender and disarmament, demobilization and reintegration*, New York: UNIFEM.

UN News Centre 2005 UN official says with autonomous government in place in Bougainville, UN mandate complete, UN News Centre, viewed 13 July 2007, <www.un.org/apps/news/story.asp?NewsID=14908&Cr=bougainvill e&Cr1>

Van Tongeren, Paul, Malin Brenk, Marte Hellema and Juliette Verhoeven 2005 *People Building Peace II*, Boulder, Colo., and London, UK: Lynne Rienner Publishers.

Vernon, Don 2005 'The Panguna mine', in Anthony J. Regan and Helga M. Griffin (eds), *Bougainville Before the Conflict*, Canberra: Pandanus Books.

Walter, Barbara 2002 *Committing to Peace: The successful settlement of civil wars*, Princeton, NJ: Princeton University Press.

Wanek, Alexander 1996 *The State and its Enemies in Papua New Guinea*, Surrey: Curzon Press.

Watts, Max 1999 'The performance of the Australian media in the Bougainville war', in Geoff Harris, Naihuwo Ahai and Rebecca Spence (eds), *Building Peace in Bougainville*, Armidale, NSW, and Waigani, PNG: The Centre for Peace Studies, University of New England and National Research Institute.

Weeks, Alan 1999 'The Bougainville peace process: an evaluation', in Geoff Harris, Naihuwo Ahai and Rebecca Spence (eds), *Building Peace in Bougainville*, Armidale, NSW, and Waigani, PNG: The Centre for Peace Studies, University of New England and National Research Institute.

Wolfers, Edward P. 2002 '"Joint creation": the Bougainville peace agreement— and beyond', *Conciliation Resources*, viewed 2 July 2007, <www.c-r.org/our-work/accord/png-bougainville/joint-creation.php>

Wolfers, Edward P. 2006a *Bougainville autonomy—implications for governance and decentralisation*, Public Policy in Papua New Guinea Discussion Paper Series No. 5, Canberra: The Australian National University,

Wolfers, Edward P. 2006b International peace missions in Bougainville, Papua New Guinea, 1990–2005—host state perspectives, Paper presented to Regional Forum on Reinventing Government, Nadi, Fiji, 20–22 February 2006.

Wolfers, Edward P. 2008 'Spotlight on mining as Autonomous Bougainville Government pursues transfer of powers and autonomy', *Papua New Guinea Yearbook*, Port Moresby.

Zale, D. 1997 *Women and the war, life issues, refugees, peace and justice*, Women Speak Out on Bougainville Forum Papers, Neutral Bay, NSW: Women for Bougainville.

Index

Abigail, Brigadier Peter 35
Aceh 5, 60, 125, 129
actors
    key peacemaking 104, 106–7, 114–19
    key war-making 104, 106, 114–19
Afghanistan 49, 120, 122, 126
Africa 2n.1, 41n.2, 49 *see also* South
    Africa
Aga, Willie 64n.6
Ahai, Naihuwo Garry 80
aid 39, 42, 44, 52, 59, 90, 105, 108, 120,
    121, 127
Alpers, Philip 64
amnesties 32, 33, 39, 62, 76, 91
Amnesty International 27, 33, 87n.2,
    87n.3
anomie 103, 106, 108
anti-mercenary norm 2n.1, 45, 49
Arawa 14n.4, 23, 24, 29, 33, 69, 78, 122,
    123
    peace ceremony (1989) 26
    Peace Conference (1994) 35–6, 37, 38,
    40, 69, 116, 131, 132
    Women's Training Centre 37n.1
Australia 2n.1, 3, 14, 15, 16, 17, 21, 23,
    30, 43, 44, 54, 55, 57, 83, 84, 85, 93,
    114, 120, 138, 139
    assistance 62, 77, 78n.3, 90, 121, 124
    colonialism 9, 10, 11–12, 16n.5, 83,
    100, 110, 112
    Defence Cooperation Program 30
    Defence Department 42
    diplomacy 48, 53, 116, 128, 139
    military 9, 26, 30, 31, 51, 53, 54, 64,
    85–6, 109–10, 116, 132
    peacekeeping 35, 51, 53, 76, 129
    peacemaking 39, 59n.5, 83, 84, 118–
    19
    police 96, 119–20
    see also weapons

Australian Agency for International
    Development (AusAID) 79, 90, 119,
    125
Autonomous Bougainville Government
    (ABG) vii, viii, 2, 9, 40, 54, 56, 58, 59,
    62, 64n.6, 76, 121, 127, 138
autonomy 2, 26, 29, 39, 56, 57, 59, 63
Avei, Moi 58, 104, 106, 115
Axelrod, Robert 132
Bailey, Jackie 62
Bana 70, 99, 100
banking system 27, 58, 90, 91, 92 *see also*
    micro-finance
Barnes, Charles (Ceb) 15, 17
Barnett, Michael 134
Barter Peace Plan 37, 46, 48, 115
Barter, Sir Peter vii, 37, 46, 49, 58, 104,
    106, 115, 116
big-manship 11, 96–9, 114, 126
Bika, John 26, 72, 116
Billy Hilly, Francis 34, 35, 104, 107
'blackbirding' 109
Bobby, Paul 41, 42
Boege, Volker 1, 30, 32, 40, 64n.6, 68, 79,
    122, 130, 131
Bougainville
    blockade 27, 28, 32, 87, 88, 92, 123
    Constituent Assembly 58
    Constitution 56, 58, 78, 120, 134
    Constitutional Commission 58, 77, 122
    House of Representatives 78, 79
    Interim Government (BIG) 28, 29, 31,
    32, 34, 39, 44, 47, 51
    Interim Provincial Government of 13,
    17n.7
    Transitional Government (BTG) 16,
    38–40, 46, 130
    see also Autonomous Bougainville
    Government, independence, Papua
    New Guinea—status of Bougainville
Bougainville Copper Agreement 14, 19
Bougainville Copper Limited (BCL) 12–
    21, 23, 27, 43, 80, 103, 106, 111, 114,
    122, 128
'Bougainville Freedom Fighters' 91, 126

www.ingramcontent.com/pod-product-compliance
Lightning Source LLC
Chambersburg PA
CBHW061240270326

41927CB00035B/3456